A publication of Brookview School
501 Zollar Drive
Benton Harbor, MI 49022

First edition, 2010

For information about special discounts for bulk purchases,
please contact the school at 269-925-3544
or see our website at www.brookviewschool.org

Book design by Carlos Albino
Cover design by Tom Allen

Map by Caroline Spikner, Brookview student

Printed by Batson Printing, Benton Harbor, Berrien County, Michigan.

ISBN: 978-0-615-37497-0

Acknowledgements

The Family Guide to Berrien County was made possible
with the generous support of:

Berrien Community Foundation
Great Lakes Heart & Vascular Institute: Dr. Thomas Pow
Lakeshore Cardiothoracic and Vascular Surgery: Dr. Kourosh Baghelai
Lake Michigan Nephrology: Drs. Daniel Brash and Oliver Songlingco

Barrett and Driscoll Pediatrics: Drs. David Driscoll and Prudie Barrett
Oncology Care Associates: Dr. Eric Lester

Thank you for purchasing the Family Guide to Berrien County! This project was started in the fall of 2009. We wanted a fundraiser that would benefit not just our school, but the community at large. Morning drop-off at Brookview is often a time to chat with other parents and hear about the weekend's activities. We realized that Brookview parents were always finding cool places and events, and wanted to share these with a wider audience. We also wanted the small local businesses that we love to grow and thrive. By writing and printing the Guide, we can share our accumulated experience of the best of Berrien County, while ensuring that Montessori education continues at Brookview for many years to come.

Our guidebook is entirely independent, written by parents, for parents. In these pages, we'll tell you everything you need to know to have a terrific time. We've covered attractions for kids ranging from toddler to teen. To make it easy for you, we've included full contact information, hours of operation, and directions. Our researchers have highlighted the best details and provided inside information on parking, bathrooms, and meals. Whether you're a visitor or a long-time resident, we think you'll find the Guide a helpful resource for your family to get the most out of your leisure time.

There are some things to keep in mind as you delve into the Guide. While we have covered all parts of Berrien County, there are a large number of attractions in downtown St. Joseph. Directions to these have been omitted to save space. Although every effort has been made to ensure accuracy, businesses come and go, and typos can happen. Call ahead to confirm key details before you leave. Also, we have tried to include a wide range of attractions, based on parental recommendations. Their inclusion in the Guide reflects individual experiences, and no endorsement by Brookview School is made or implied. Finally, we realize that no guidebook can be entirely comprehensive. If you think we've missed something important, we'd love to hear about it! Please submit feedback through our website at brookviewschool.org. While we can't answer each message individually, we will be using all of them to update future editions of the Guide.

As usual at Brookview, there were lots of contributors to the Guide as the project continued through the 2009 - 2010 school year. Julia Gourley and Tamara Samuels were early champions, and kept it on track as tasks multiplied. Jenny Stirling did a market analysis that helped determine the feasibility of the project. Hollie Blakeney provided early style guidelines and editing.

Introduction (cont.)

Carlos Albino designed the interior pages and did all the layout. Tom Allen crafted the cover art. The list of writers who contributed is very long, but Juan Ganum, who took on many of the south county topics, deserves a special mention. Nina Davis, Elena Fuller and Polya Samardar's work did not make it into this edition of the Guide, but their efforts laid a good foundation for our second edition. Chris Kwon ran the online wiki where our collaborative efforts took place. Beth Peace, Susan Westin and Lorrie Kuhns went through the manuscript with an eagle eye. Larry Schanker contributed many of the chapter introductions, sharing his Montessori expertise. Leslie Sullivan also penned some introductory material, and with Julee Laurent worked on promoting the book throughout the county and beyond.

If you would like to learn more about Brookview, please call or write to arrange a tour. We're very proud of our school and would love to show you all the wonderful learning that takes place there every day. On behalf of all the Brookview families, please enjoy the Family Guide to Berrien County with our best wishes.

Sincerely,
Katie Westin Kwon
Editor-in-chief

Writers

Michelle Allen
Alloyd Blackmon
Hollie Blakeney
Sue Dubar
Kristin Emanuel
Kristin Fatouros
Amy Frieden
Scott Fuller
Jody Ganum
Juan Ganum
Cara Gillespie
Julia Gourley
Joey Greene
Bill Korbel
Laura Korbel
Lorrie Kuhns
Katie Kwon
Ed Lau
Jody Lau
Colleen Liotine
Irma Marrero
Sylvia Moreira
Mark Moreno
Larry Prange
Emily Rusk
Larry Schanker
Anna Schelling
Jennifer Spikner
Leslie Sullivan
Kate Terrell
Dawn Tomlinson
Claire Thrum
Marc Thrum

INTRODUCTION

We can't say enough great things about our county libraries and bookstores. The libraries offer an incredible range of services and resources for the entire community, and all on a limited budget. Our local bookstores are run by people motivated by love of the printed word who are eager to share that love with others. Brookview students share that love, and the classrooms are well-stocked with books. It's not uncommon to see a three year old in Primary seek out an older child to read a book together. Our library is housed in the Great Room, the heart of the school, where our students perform, study, meet and organize. We encourage everyone to support our local libraries and bookstores to keep them strong and vibrant members of our community.

Berrien Springs Community Library

215 W. Union Street
Berrien Springs, MI 49103
269-471-7074
www.bsclibrary.org

Monday - Thursday 10 am - 8 pm
Friday 10 am - 6 pm
Saturday 10 am - 4 pm
Closed Sundays

The Berrien Springs Community Library is a popular meeting place for kids at the end of the school day. Part of the draw is the large and well-appointed children's section, located directly to your right as you enter. There are a number of computers, equipped with headphones for listening to audiobooks, as well as Internet access. Inside the children's section, comfortable window seats invite readers to curl up with a book. The library has two story hours each week, with a target audience of five and under. Generally, these are on Tuesdays at 1:30 pm and Thursdays at 11 am, but up-to-date times are available on their website. Story time takes place inside the special barn structure inside the children's section, and usually consists of two or three stories, a craft and a snack. There is also a monthly Craft Day for elementary students and their parents to participate in together.

The library is closed if Berrien Springs schools are closed for inclement weather.

Berrien Springs Community Library (cont.)

Directions: From US-31, take exit 15A, Old 31/M-139, into the Village of Berrien Springs. The library is on your right as you enter town, and visible from the road. Turn right onto Union Street for parking.

Buffalo Books

120 W. Buffalo St.
New Buffalo, MI 49117
269-231-5300

Summer hours:
Wednesday - Friday 12 noon - 6 pm
Saturday 10 am - 6 pm
Sunday 10 am - 4 pm

Winter hours:
Wednesday - Friday 1 pm - 6 pm
Saturday 11 am - 6 pm
Sunday 11 am - 3 pm

Buffalo Books may be relatively new on the scene, but it already feels like an established neighborhood treasure. The cozy, rambling store has wood floors and books tucked away in snug corners. There is a separate young adult section which averages 150-200 titles, while the children's section carries books for toddlers through fifth grade. The proprietors have a background in the arts, so they seek out the best new books in children's literature, focusing on well-told, beautifully illustrated volumes. If you're looking for something special, they can have any in-print book within 24 to 48 hours.

Buffalo Books includes a custom clothing store and an art gallery on the scond level. They are planning on expanding their section on local and state history. Also, they have a community meeting space that is available to local groups without charge. Connected to the bookstore through a door, the space has armchairs, a fireplace, and a ping-pong table. A reading circle for preschoolers meets here on Thursdays from 2 - 2:30 pm. The owners will read a few books while parents have the chance to browse the store. Teachers receive a 10% discount at Buffalo Books.

Directions: From I-94, take exit 4B, New Buffalo, onto West Pulaski Highway, also called US-12. The street becomes West Buffalo St as you enter the town; Buffalo Books is on your right. There is a small parking lot behind the store.

Forever Books

312 State Street
St. Joseph, MI 49085
269-982-1110
www.foreverbooks.net

Winter Hours:
Monday - Saturday 10 am - 6 pm
Friday 10 am - 8 pm
Sunday 11 am - 5 pm

Summer hours:
Monday - Saturday 10 am - 8 pm
Sunday 11 am - 5 pm

For the last ten years, Forever Books has provided Berrien County with excellent reading material. It is a store run by and directed at book lovers, and it shows in the thoughtful selection. The children's material takes up the entire back section of the store. Choices start with the bright and colorful board books, and expand into a shelf of picture books. There's a significant commitment to diversity and a refreshing lack of television and toy spin-offs. This is the place to go for hardcover editions of children's classics that you'll want for your child's library. Older readers will enjoy several shelves of series and young adult novels.

The children's section is decorated with displays highlighting favorite books - on a recent trip, we saw Peter Rabbit, Where the Wild Things Are, and the works of Mo Willens. One wall is dedicated to crafts and hobby books. There is a small assortment of quality toys that tie into the books on display. In the very back is a small nook with kid-sized chairs and a table to keep children busy while you browse. Forever Books offers a free gift wrapping service, so this is also a great place to pick up a birthday or holiday present.

Lakeside Books

Lakeside Books
222 N Paw Paw St.
Coloma, MI 49038
269-468-4117
www.lakesidebooks.com

Monday - Saturday 10 am - 8 pm
Closed Sundays

Lakeside Books (cont.)

Retail bookstores offer a terrific selection of the latest releases. Used bookstores let you scoop up treasures at a fraction of the cover price. Get the best of both worlds at Lakeside Books in downtown Coloma. The bulk of the inventory is used books. These are arranged neatly on the tall wood shelves that line the perimeter of the store, and sell for 50 - 75% off the retail price. They also carry all the current bestsellers, and their standard pricing is 15% off the cover. DVD's, audiobooks, and an extensive children's section round out the store. Curl up in one of the cozy armchairs, and enjoy some free coffee and cookies while you browse. There are a few colorful fish tanks tucked in between the shelves.

The storefront holds only a fraction of their extensive inventory, but you can search everything they have at their website. If you nee something that's not currently in stock, they can order it for you right away. Lakeside Books acquires books through estate sales and donations. A portion of the sales from donated books goes to Coloma schools. We're excited to see another independent bookstore in Berrien County.

Directions: From I-94, take exit 39 towards Millburg/Coloma. Travel north on Church St, which becomes N Paw Paw St. Lakeside Books will be on your left.

Maud Preston Palenske Library

500 Market Street
Saint Joseph, MI 49085
269-983-7167
www.youseemore.com/maudpreston

Monday - Thursday 10 am - 9 pm
Friday - Saturday 10 am - 6 pm

This friendly library strives to offer something for every age group. The main floor features reading materials for adults, a wide selection of audio and video recordings, a computer center, a geneology studies room, and a quiet, sun-filled reading room. Just inside the main doors and to the left you will find the teen-only room. Head downstairs and enter the delightful chidlren's library.

The library's teen program rivals other popular after-school and out-of-school activities for this age group. Teens enjoy video and board game competitions,

Maud Preston Palenske (cont.)

t-shirt re-makes, book groups and so much more. The young librarians who oversee this program are tons of fun and rightfully deserve the respect the teens give them. The teen room is a sacred place. Do not mistake this as a quiet room where you can read with your preschooler. You will politely be asked to relocate to another area of the library.

The Children's Library is downstairs. At both entrances you find temptations lurking including a wooden train track and puppets on one side and a table with puzzles and make-and-take activities on the other. The front area offers comfy seating so you may enjoy your new novel while your child catches up on play time. This area also features most of the collection of picture books and a selection of audio and video recordings. All media in the Children's Library are free to check out. The back of the room features weekly story times for babies, toddlers, preschoolers, and elementary-age children. Call the Library for details on days and times. Some programs like the Bouncing Babies to Books require advance registration.

Niles District Library

620 East Main Street
Niles, MI 49120
269-683-8545
www.nileslibary.com

Monday - Thursday 9 am - 8 pm
Friday - Saturday 9 am - 5 pm
Closed Sundays

The Niles Library serves childen from infant age through high school with two separate sections in its large, sunlit building. When you enter the library, the "Children's Depot" is on your left. This section of the library is designed for children up through fifth grade. The train decor reflects the importance of railroads in the history of Niles. Look up when you enter this section to see a hand-painted mural of the surrounding countryside and a model railroad running along a special see-through shelf. Ask the librarians at the children's desk and they will set the train in motion. Bean bag chairs, armchairs, and low tables provide places to read and study. There are no Internet terminals here, but the workstations allow older children to check the card catalog, as well as access to their school reading lists. The shelves are all topped with a huge

Niles District Library (cont.)

selection of stuffed animals, although they are not to be touched, which could provoke fussing from some younger children.

At the back of the Depot is the story time room; the floor is covered with bright mats that make for more comfortable sitting. This is the gathering place for the Squigglers, a weekly session deisgned for infants up to age thirty months. Squigglers meets each Wednesday after preschool storytime, and the meetings include active plays, music, rhymes and exercises chosen with a short attention span in mind. Outside the storytime room is an area for toddlers, with board books and puzzles, as well as some extra floor space. Please note, the Depot does connect to the adult stacks at the back, on the left, so parents need to be aware their younger children can wander away.

Older children can join the Chess Club or the Junior Garden Club, both of which meet regularly at the library. Middle schoolers can find YA (young adult) literature in their own section, located directly to your right on entry. "Castaway Cove" has a tiki bar and some cabana furniture where readers can browse. Finally, the Niles library has a special collection on local history and genealogy. This collection is housed in two rooms next to the YA section, and is open for limited hours. Wireless internet access is available throughout the library - get the login at the circulation desk.

Directions: From US-31, take exit 5, Niles-Buchanan Rd, towards Niles. Enter the city of Niles and cross the river - the road becomes Broadway. Make a left on 7th St and an immediate left on Cedar St. Access to the library parking lot is on the right.

Stevensville Library

Lincoln Township Public Library
2099 W. John Beers Road
Stevensville, MI 49127
269-429-9575
www.lincolntownshiplibrary.org

Monday - Thursday 10 am - 9pm
Friday - Saturday 10 am - 5 pm

Stevensville's library is notable for its new, bright and airy building. The children's section is located on the first floor and takes up about the third of the

Stevensville Library (cont.)

space. The thoughtful layout gives kids of varying ages their own spaces. Toddlers like the coloring table and the story time room, where walls are painted to resemble a fairy tale cottage. Outside the cottage door is a tree that is decorated to reflect the changing seasons. Smaller children have their own right-sized toilet and sink within their designated children's bathrooms. Several listening stations allow children to enjoy the large selection of books on tape, as well as music CDs.

The middle of the children's section holds a cluster of computers with Internet access. The computers are also loaded with age-appropriate games and learning resources. The Lincoln Township website is an outstanding resource for families. Here you can find links to online learning sites, homeschool curricula, reading lists from local schools, and book suggestions from organizations across the country.

Story times are very well run and offer a range of experiences. Some are age restricted and require advance sign-up, which is done by phone. The times and dates are announced in advance on the library website. The "Just Threes" time is very popular, as parents are not allowed in the story time room, and have to find ways to occupy themselves within the library for thirty minutes or so. The library also offers several drop-in story hours throughout the week. There's a bedtime story hour on Monday nights at 7 pm which includes both stories and a craft.

Tweens (grades 4 - 6) have their own book club as they learn to appreciate more advanced literature. For older kids, the teen advisory board helps plan the many activities that the library offers to teens, including game nights, book clubs and an annual lock-in. Teens have their own section of the library website with links to music and game sites, as well as reviews of books from book club members.

Directions: From I-94, take exit 22 and travel east on W John Beers Rd. You will find the library on the north side of W John Beers Rd, between Red Arrow Highway and Cleveland Ave.

NOTES:

INTRODUCTION

Education using hands-on materials and experiential activities is a cornerstone of Montessori philosophy. We also try and provide extensions to the curriculum for those students who are especially inspired by a particular subject area. The museums in our region provide fertile ground for these extensions, not only for field trips from school, but for families to use as part of their own learning environment. From science to art to history, enjoy the child-friendly exhibits of our local museums and galleries.

Box Factory for the Arts

1101 Broad Street
Saint Joseph, MI 49085
269-983-3688
www.boxfactoryforthearts.org

Monday - Saturday 10 am - 4 pm
Concerts Saturday night at 8 pm
Sunday 1 pm - 4 pm

The Box Factory is the home of the Berrien Artists Guild, which is a non-profit organization consisting of local artists, writers, film makers, actors and patrons. Art lessons are available along with writing workshops. These are great opportunities to expand your horizons.

The building was originally a box factory, thus the name. It is located just east of downtown Saint Joseph with ample parking across the street. The building alone is a great reason to go. It has massive beams and rustic wood floors which add to the ambiance. You'll find studios throughout the facility where artists are working and exhibit their work. If you find something you would like to buy and the artist is not in, simply go to the volunteer at the front desk to make your purchase. You'll also find books, CDs and DVDs from local talent on sale. The gift shop has many beautiful and exciting items as well.

Exhibits are always changing, and include works from local and regional artists as well as students. They host a variety of concerts and special performances, usually at 8 pm on Saturday nights. Tickets are reasonably priced. Their class schedule is posted on their website and includes classes for middle school

Box Factory for the Arts (cont.)

and high school students. They have recently added a theater workshop that will run during the summer, as well as some filmmaking courses.

Directions: From Main St in St. Joseph, turn onto Broad St, traveling away from the lake. The Box Factory is on your left, just after you cross Wayne St.

Buchanan Art Center

117 W. Front Street
Buchanan, MI 49107
269-697-4005
www.buchananartcenter.org

Monday - Wednesday 9 am - 6 pm
Thursday 10 am - 6 pm
Friday 10 am - 5 pm
Saturday 10 am - 4 pm
Sunday (summers only) 1 pm - 4 pm

The Buchanan Art Center is easily spotted as you drive up Front Street - there's a sculpted giraffe in the front yard, stretching up to nibble on a dogwood tree. Other outdoor sculptures on display include a pair of white whooping cranes, a heron with a fish, and a tiger crouching in the black-eyed susans. When you walk inside, the first of three galleries will be on your left. The Buchanan Art Center displays the works of local artists in a variety of media. New exhibits are staged every six weeks.

The center offers classes for kids as young as three, who start with "Scribble Worms." There are open studio hours, but kids must have taken a class first in order to participate. The center is well equipped for all types of artistic work. They have a pottery studio with nine wheels, a clay roller, and four kilns. There's a large work space for painters, drawers and printmakers. Once a year they hold a juried art show, open to entries in all media types and from all ages. The 2009 show was "Mythological Creatures" and the topic changes every year.

There is a selection of art books available for further study. Some of the gallery exhibits include works that can be purchased. There is also a gift shop in the front of the store, where crafts such as knitting, woodworking, jewelry and pottery are for sale.

Buchanan Art Center (cont.)

Directions: From US-31, take exit 5, Niles-Buchanan Rd, towards Buchanan. It becomes Front St as you enter Buchanan, after travelling about 1 1/2 miles. The art center is on your left, another 1/2 mile up Front St.

Chartreuse

304 State Street
St. Joseph, Michigan 49085
269-983-0931
www.chartreuseartgallery.com

Summer hours (Memorial day - early October):
Monday - Thursday 10 am - 6 pm
Friday and Saturday 10 am - 8 pm
Sunday noon - 5 pm

Winter hours:
Monday, Thursday and Saturday 11 am - 6 pm
Friday 11 am - 8 pm
Sunday 11 - 4
Closed Tuesday and Wednesday
Extended hours beofre Christmas

Chartreuse is an artist-owned and operated gallery located in downtown St. Joseph. The gallery features beautiful artisan pieces in all types of mediums – ceramic, fiber, glass/metal, jewelry, painting, drawings, photography and wood – against chartreuse-hued walls. It's well-worth wandering through the entire gallery, although small kids may have a hard time keeping their hands away from fragile pieces.

Artists that live within 50 miles of St. Joseph are welcome to apply. Because it is a co-operative, Chartreuse offers the local artists' work directly to shoppers at fair prices. They strive to have something to offer at all price points, from small gifts under $10 all the way to large paintings. Many of the works are inspired by the beautiful scenery of Berrien County, making Chartreuse an excellent place to pick up a unique keepsake. The artist members all take turns working at the gallery, so customers get a chance to meet them and talk about their work.

Curious Kids Museum

415 Lake Blvd.
St. Joseph MI 49085
269-983-2543
www.curiouskidsmuseum.org

Curious Kids Discovery Zone

333 Broad St.
St. Joseph MI 49085
269-982-8500

Winter Hours:
Wednesday - Saturday 10 am - 5 pm
(Discovery Zone closed Wednesday)
Sunday noon - 5 pm

Summer Hours:
Monday - Saturday 10 am - 5 pm
Sunday noon - 5 pm

The Curious Kids Museum's main building is on the bluff overlooking Lake Michigan in downtown Saint Joseph. This is a top destination for families throughout the year. In winter, it's the perfect place to get out of the house and burn off some energy. In the summers, the museum gets especially busy any time rain or wind drives visitors off the beach. The museum is thoughtfully laid out to create spaces for small groups to play. The entrance has racks for coats and a small gift shop. There is only limited room for stroller parking. The downstairs is popular with smaller children. In the main hallway is a rotating exhibit that highlights life in different countries throughout the world; smaller kids love to play "house" and dress the part. To the right is the extremely popular face-painting station. The face paint markers are very high quality and you can purchase your own set to take home at the gift shop. Beyond the face painting, kids under five have the spacious "Toddle Farm" to themselves. Make sure toddlers wear the protective aprons as they play in the water feature, as they can get wet very quickly at this station. There is a private corner for breastfeeding mothers behind the large play barn.

Further back on the first floor, take a slide down the side of an erupting volcano or explore the rain forest. Whatever you do, don't miss the apple picking exhibit at the very back. Kids from two to ten work together to collect apples from the trees against the wall. They're loaded into the hopper and, with a turn of the wheel, the apples are lifted up to the ceiling, where they tumble down chutes and magically appear again on the trees. A wheelbarrow and picking baskets add to the fun. The back of the museum is also where you can find the bathrooms, water fountains, and elevator to the second floor.

Curious Kids Museum (cont.)

The upper level of the museum focuses more on science and technology. This region is particularly well-suited to older children. Highlights include the chance to stand inside a soap bubble, a wheelchair obstacle course, and the chance to participate in a space shuttle launch. Recent exhibits have also allowed children the chance to appear as TV newscasters and to "freeze" their shadows on a screen. This is a larger space with lots of tall exhibits, and it can be easy to lose sight of smaller children for a few moments at a time. Still, they enjoy the chance to play the tube organ with flip-flops (provided) or check out the back of an ambulance. Station one adult by the staircase and one by the elevator, and you won't lose anyone.

Starting in January 2010, the Discovery Zone has been open for fun. This is located in the Silver Beach complex, which also houses the Carousel and the Shadowlands ballroom. The Discovery Zone requires a separate admission charge. Permanent exhibits include the rock climbing wall and the water table, where kids can try to maneuver toy boats using currents and wind cannons. There will also be a rotating selection of exhibits, with details available on the website. For smaller children, we're not entirely convinced the extra admission charge to the Discovery Zone is worth it. Benefactor families ($130/year) get free admission to both the main museum and the Discovery Zone; anyone spending more than a week or two per year in Berrien County should consider purchasing a membership.

Fort St. Joseph Museum

508 E. Main Street
Niles, MI 49120
269-683-4702 ext 236
www.fortstjosephmuseum.org

Wednesday - Friday 10 am - 4 pm
Saturday 10 am - 3 pm

The exterior of the Fort St. Joseph Museum in Niles looks just as a museum should. It's housed in what was once the carriage house of the wonderfully ornate Chapin Mansion. The mansion proper now serves as Niles' City Hall, while the carriage house holds a delightful treasure trove of historical and social exhibits spanning all of Niles' rich history.

Fort St. Joseph Museum (cont.)

The lower floor holds the historical collection, with four main areas of interest. These cover the ongoing archaeological work at the Fort St. Joseph dig, the Underground Railroad, a collection of Lakota Indian artifacts, and an exhibit on the railroad classification yards that played a major role in Niles' early industrial days. You can see actual pieces, over 350 years old, including religious medallions the early French explorers gave to the Native American people, and soldiers' buckles and buttons from the fort. One of the crown jewels in the museum collection is a series of hand-drawn pictographs done by Sitting Bull. In 2008, a Native American artist made copies of these rare drawings for the Little Bighorn Museum in Montana; the originals remain in Niles. Only four of the twelve are on display at any one time, in order to help preserve them. Local Niles history is also showcased with a detailed plat map from 1837, and the register from the Niles Hotel, dated 1926. Look for the signature of Mr. and Mrs. J. Klock of Benton Harbor - they donated the land for Jean Klock Park in memory of their daughter. On the right side of the museum, you'll find the first printing press to be brought to Niles.

Upstairs, the exhibits focus on daily life of Niles residents from pioneer times to the modern era. Niles has some fantastic architecture, and there's a pictorial display of all the different styles of houses in the city. There are a series of miniature rooms made by Michigan resident Emma Rodgers, and a giant loom once used to weave bolts of cloth. It's fun to look at memorabilia from local clubs, baseball teams, medical providers (including the legendary Dr. Bonine, an eye specialist), police and fire departments, and schools. One wall showcases relics from veterans from the Civil War to Vietnam. There's a special section on local literary hero Ring Lardner, one of the most popular writers of the 1920's. Children love the two-headed lamb, a popular display item for many decades.

The museum now offers monthly children's activities, including a scavenger hunt, activity booklet and craft suggestions. Brochures are age-specific and available for free at the front desk. They are attractively printed in full color so that even pre-readers can use the pictures to search their way through the museum.

City Hall, housed in the Chapin Mansion, is adjacent to the museum. Step inside - you can see the detailed woodwork, stained glass, and elaborately carved fireplace mantel, as well as hand-stenciled ceilings. City Hall workers welcome you to walk into any room not in active use.

Fort St. Joseph Museum (cont.)

Directions: From US-31, take exit 5, the Niles-Buchanan Road, towards Niles. Cross the river; the street name changes to Broadway. Make a left on 5th St. The City Hall and Museum will be two blocks up on your right, at the intersection of 5th and Main.

The Heritage Museum and Cultural Center

601 Main Street
St. Joseph, MI 49085
269-983-1191
www.theheritagemcc.org

Tuesday - Saturday: 10 am - 4 pm year-round
June - September: also open Sundays noon - 4 pm

The Priscilla U. Byrns Heritage Center in downtown St. Joseph houses exhibit halls, artifact and archival collections, a research library, and elegant banquet facilities, and is the home of The Heritage Museum and Cultural Center. Their mission is to promote historical preservation, education, and research that relates to Benton Harbor, St. Joseph and the surrounding region. It is a wonderful place to visit. The exhibits are beautifully organized, with large panels of information along with interesting artifacts and documentation, in a flowing, family-friendly context.

One recent exhibit was entitled The French in North America/Les Francais en Amerique du Nord--An Enduring Presence. It examined the history of the French Empire on this continent and included artifacts from an archaeology project at Fort St. Joseph. Other exhibits have included The Working Waterfront, which was a celebration of maritime traditions in the local area, an exhibit of the extensive China Collection of the Heritage Museum, and an exhibit that explored two different shipwrecks that occured off the coast of South Haven, MI, in 1891 and 1902.

The Research Library of the Heritage Museum includes books about local history by local authors, postcards and photo collections, maps, and much more. In addition, the Center houses collections of slides, tapes containing oral histories of local citizens, and geneological records. To round out the Heritage Center's offerings, beautiful facilities are available for rent for weddings, parties, meetings, and concerts. We particularly love the sound of the 9-foot Baldwin concert grand piano in Shephard Hall, the largest space at the Center. There can be no better place to learn about the history of this beautiful lakefront region.

Horn Archaeological Museum and Museum of Natural History

Andrews University
9047 US-31
Berrien Springs, MI 49014
269-471-3273
www.andrews.edu/archaeology

Hours: You're on your own.

All right, we've given you the inside scoop throughout the Guide. However, in the eight months it took to write this book, there was one nut we couldn't crack. Andrews University has not one, but two interesting little museums sequestered away on its grounds. Or so we hear. We have not been successful in actually getting inside. However, we thought we'd include them as a challenge to families. Their collections are so unexpected, we think they might be worth seeking out.

Here's what we know. The Siegfried Horn Museum of Archaeology is currently undergoing renovation. It will be occupying a brown building right next to Apple Valley Supermarket, and indeed there is a nice sign out front on US-31. The collection includes almost 3,000 cuneiform tablets spanning Sumerian through Neo-Babylonian times. There are also artifacts from the Holy Land, including coins, jewelry, pottery, tools and weapons. Andrews students and professors continue to work on digs in Jordan and other middle Eastern countries, so the museum's collection is always expanding. The Horn Museum hosts lectures given by distinguished archaeologists from around the world. Hopefully, once they are well-established in their new home, they will be more accessible. We think this is a great local resource for those interested in archaeology.

Price Hall is part of the science complex on Andrews' campus. The lower level contains the Museum of Natural History. This is a large collection of botanical and animal specimens, including shells, plants, birds and insects. The museum's crown jewel is the Prillwitz Mammoth, the largest mammoth skeleton ever found in Michigan. It was unearthed in 1962, and was donated by the Prillwitz family to Andrews University. Sounds pretty cool! Let us know what you find.

Directions: From US-31, take exit 15A, M-139, into Berrien Springs. The entrance to Andrews University is very well marked on your right.

Krasl Art Center

707 Lake Boulevard
St. Joseph, MI 49085
269-983-0271
www.krasl.org

Monday - Wednesday and Friday - Saturday: 10 am - 4 pm
Thursday: 10 am - 8 pm
Sunday: 1 - 4 pm

Located at the top of the bluff from Silver Beach and just two blocks south of downtown St. Joseph sits the Krasl Art Center. Walk along Lake Bluff Park and look across Lake Boulevard at the west side of the building to enjoy the kinetic sculpure by George Rickey. People of all ages enjoy seeing how the movement of the sculpture changes with the weather. As you step inside and look up you'll see the colorful glass chandelier by artist Dale Chihuly. Don't miss driving by at night to see this sculpture, Beacon Gold, lit up year-round.

Inside are three galleries, small enough to keep the attention of young visitors, but with artwork interesting enough that adults may wish to spend a bit more time. Not to worry, most exhibitions include make-and-take activities children can work on with help from parents. During the summer months, children ages 4-15 enjoy the popular Summer Art Camps. There are also parent/child workshops, one-day classes, camps for adults and studio art experiences for all ages. The studios, including ceramics, darkroom, sculpture, and multipurpose studios are located in the lower level and on the second floor and are well-stocked with quality art materials that are not found in most home studios or at school. Teaching faculty are fun, experienced artists and teachers whose artwork is showcased in galleries throughout the region.

Throughout Berrien County, you may notice the Krasl Art Center's collection of sculptures. Pick up a SculpTour guide, Kids SculpTour guide or use the cell phone based Touch Tone Art & Culture for information about the sculptures designed for kids and adults. If you happen to be around for one of the Friday evening receptions, be sure to take advantage of the fun Kids' Art Workshops. Or check out the Family Open Studios on the second Sunday of most months - make a mess in the studio while saving your dining room table for dinner. The Krasl Art Center also offers comprehensive birthday parties. Although there are no picnic tables in the yard, families are welcome to bring a picnic blanket and enjoy the spacious, shady lawn.

The Museum at Southwestern Michigan College

58900 Cherry Grove Rd.
Dowagiac, MI 49047
269-782-1374
www.swmich.edu/museum

Tuesday - Friday 10 am - 5 pm
Saturday 11 am - 3 pm

What do children love most about this museum? Is it the secret room in the Underground Railroad exhibition, the fishing boat, holding the Potawatomi objects, climbing up the cargo net, or the recreation of Dowagiac in the 1800's including a working train yard? There are so many great opportunities for children to be engaged that you almost forget that you are visiting a museum honoring local history. Best of all, admission is free.

The four newly-renovated galleries are bright, cheery and filled with professionally displayed objects. Immediately upon entering the gallery you'll notice the scale model of Dowagiac including the train yard. On one side you'll see Dowagiac in 1920, on the other is Dowagiac in 1870. (It's fun to drive through downtown before coming to the museum and then see if you can identify the buildings as you look at the models.) Both historical renderings of the city were taken from photographs of the city. The interactive waterwheel mill is another favorite in this gallery as is the room from the Underground Railroad. The Model Smith Hoist surely won't be missed since it reaches all the way to the ceiling. Try the small model to see how this Dowagiac invention helps move loads from one place to another. Like to fish? Drop a few Heddon brand fishing lures in a fish tank to see how the different lures move in the water. Before you leave, be sure to climb the cargo net on the side of the SS Webb Miller.

Formal programs are available for scout and school groups. The campus of Southwestern Michigan College is grassy and sprawling. Bring along a picnic lunch in the summer and enjoy your surroundings. You could easily spend one or two hours in this highly interactive museum. Take a break for lunch, then head back inside to finish up in the galleries.

Directions: From I-94, take exit 29, Pipestone Rd, headed east and merge onto Meadowbrook Rd. Travel eight miles, then take a right onto MI-140S. After another 6.5 miles, make another right onto MI-62E. Make a left on Spruce St as you enter Dowagiac, then continue on Main St. Main St. becomes Division St/MI-62E and veers southeast. Make a slight right onto Cherry Grove Rd; the entrance to Southwestern Michigan College will be on your right.

New Territory Arts Association and The Studios at 210

210 Water Street
Benton Harbor, MI 49022
269-926-1926
www.newterritoryarts.org

The New Territory Arts Association (NTAA) is a group of citizens dedicated to the development of the Benton Harbor Arts District, which is an area just off Main Street in Benton Harbor. The NTAA has been instrumental in the redevelopment of restaurants, businesses and residential properties in the district.

The Studios at 210 are located in an ideal building that used to be a car dealership. The front of the building has three large glass garage doors that can be fully opened when the weather is nice. Inside, there is a bright and open gallery space and about twelve artist studios. The artists all work in their studios and the building is open whenever there are artists in the building. Although not fully established, there are regular weekend hours. Look for the sign out front to see if they are open.

The building hosts various events including fundraisers, weddings, celebrations, and art shows. Many artists teach classes and yoga classes are held on a regular basis. There are large, clean restrooms available, but no changing tables.

Directions: From I-94, take exit 33, I-94 Business/E Main St and travel 3.2 miles. Make a right on Water St. The Studios at 210 will be on your right.

North Berrien Historical Museum

300 Coloma Avenue
Coloma, MI 49038
269-468-3330
www.northberrienhistory.org

Summer (May - September):
Wednesday - Saturday, 10 am - 4 pm
Winter:
Wednesday - Friday, 10 am - 4 pm

General admission is free.

North Berrien Historical Museum (cont.)

"Are we going to the Lincoln Log museum, Mom?" This is the response we get every time we mention visiting the North Berrien Historical Museum. The museum does in fact include a log cabin as well as the Carter Centennial Farm House and Barn, Print Shop and Nichols/Beverly Agricultural Building. Year-round activities take place in and around the buildings on this four-acre museum campus.

Exhibitions in the main (Lincoln) log cabin change perodically but always reflect the museum's goal to collect, preserve and display the history of Hagar, Coloma, Watervliet and Bainbridge Townships as well as the cities of Coloma and Watervliet. Which, it turns out, is actually quite interesteing.

The out buildings are also fascinating but it can be helpful to visit them with a member of the museum's staff or a volunteer. Children seem to have more questions about farm equipment and printing presses than the average family has knowledge of. The education staff has a series of programs available for groups of children including tours and traveling trunks about Lincoln, Frontier Days, Potawatomi and 19th Century Toys and Games. Participation in these events should be arranged prior to your visit.

This museum puts on many celebrations with activities for all ages. The Holiday Open House features gingerbread house making, visits from Mr. & Mrs. Claus, workshops for children and a cookie walk. During spring and summer break children can participate in one of numerous workshops or camps. During the annual Glad Peach Festival you'll find activities and refreshments at the museum. They even publically celebrate Valentine's Day with fun activities for children.

You will find the staff in the main log cabin so always stop there first. During many festivals and events you will find this museum teeming with cookies, punch and coffee. Activities are usually drop-in but do sometimes require a small fee for participation.

Directions: From I-94, take exit 39. Turn right on Friday Rd, then left on Ryno Rd. Make a right on S. West St, followed by a left on Pearl St. Next Turn right on Sadie Ln, and then left on W. St. Joseph St. Finally, turn right on Coloma Ave. North Berrien Historical Musuem will be on the left.

Water Street Glassworks

142 Water St.
Benton Harbor, MI 49023
269-925-5555
www.waterstreetglassworks.org

September through April
Monday and Friday 2 - 6 pm
Tuesday, Wednesday and Thursday 10 am - 2 pm

May - August
also Saturday 11 am - 6 pm and Sunday noon - 5 pm

Located in the Historic Hinkley buidling, this working glass studio is a joy to stumble upon. Just blocks from the Benton Harbor Public Library and The Livery, it is a must-see destination during a visit to the Benton Harbor Arts District. The main entrance is sometimes locked, so take the time to stroll around to the back door to see if they are in. The main floor includes the gallery at the front, office at the back and the catwalk overlooking the glass-blowing facility. If you happen upon a reception or class, the folks at Water Street will invite you to sidle up to the railing at the catwalk to see the artists at work. Even in the middle of winter this space can be HOT so be prepared to shed layers!

Water Street Glassworks offers glass and metal working classes for teens and adults. Their successful Fired Up program offers glass programming for teens during the after school hours. The Fired Up students almost always have art-work for sale in the office. It's worth a look.

Directions: From I-94, take exit 33, I-94 Bus W/ E Main St and travel 3.2 miles. Turn right on Water St; the glassworks will be on your right.

NOTES:

INTRODUCTION

From a very young age, Brookview students are exposed to music from all the world's cultures including the canon, of western classical music. We also allow opportunities for theatrical performances, of Shakespeare, folk tales, and even original works written by the children. There is no better way to capitalize on this exposure than to expose children to a variety of live performances. Sometimes the child will be inspired by the musical or dramatic work, and sometimes going to a concert or theatrical performance will be about the experience of enjoying the arts as a community. Either way, Southwest Michigan offers a multitude of choices to enjoy.

Acorn Theater

107 Generations Drive
Three Oaks, MI 49128
269-756-3879
www.acorntheater.com

Shows most Friday and Saturdays, as well as events during the week

The Acorn Theater is located in arts-loving Three Oaks. This tiny town (less than 2000 inhabitants) has a vibrant, thriving arts scene, and the Acorn is one of the lead participants. The theater seats 250 people and has an intimate, cozy feel. They have a wide variety of performances, including singers and musicians, classic movies, opera, magic shows and more. If you're on Facebook, become a "fan" as they periodically post announcements about the more kid-friendly shows. There is a wine shop attached to the theater that serves as additional gallery space to showcase local artists; they carry craft beers, reasonably priced wines, and some unique gifts. Tickets for the shows can be purchased through the website; call the box office for reservations.

Directions: From I-94, take exit 12 toward Sawyer onto Sawyer Rd. Take the third left onto Three Oaks Rd, which becomes Elm St. Make a right onto Generations Dr (this is a very small street) to get to the theater.

Brown Bag Concert Series

Howard Band Shell
Corner of Lake Boulevard and Port Street
269-985-1111
www.sjtoday.org

Wednesdays noon to 1:00 pm
Mid-June through August
Rain dates are Thursday

The Brown Bag Concert series is a wonderful free outdoor musical event for the entire family. Each week brings new performances from local and regional musicians. From woodwind quintets, solo guitarists, folk singers, choirs, light jazz, blues, and kids' music, all make for a very entertaining lunch break in the sun. If it is sunny, bring the sunscreen. There is a limited amount of shade, mostly in the grassy areas, so arrive early if you want shade. Otherwise the John E. N. Howard Band Shell is an ideal location for the concert series. Lake Michigan is in the background and the St. Joseph River runs close by allowing for the occasional glimpse of boat traffic. It's walking distance from downtown, which offers you the opportunity pick up a take-out lunch from various eateries.

The venue is wheelchair accessible and stroller-friendly. Port Street is closed off to automobile traffic for the event but parking is plentiful, either on side streets or the various public parking lots near by.

After the concert, from 1:00 pm to 3:00 pm, there are free horse drawn trolley tours starting in front of The Welcome Center at 120 State Street. A large Percheron horse pulls the trolley through the streets of historic downtown St. Joseph. You can also stroll a little further down State Street to Kilwin's for an ice cream, making an ideal finish to a wonderful event.

Celebration! Cinema

1468 Cinema Way
Benton Harbor, MI 49022
269-934-7469
www.celebrationcinema.com - select Benton Harbor location

Open daily; movies start at 11 am

Celebration! Cinema (cont.)

All the latest releases are playing at Celebration! Cinema, a multi-screen digital format theater. Everyone gets a great seat in the comfortable stadium-style chairs. Popular movies often show on multiple screens, making it likely you will see your movie when you want. We love that you can purchase tickets online, minimizing wait times with squirmy children. Their lobby is clean, spacious and comfortable, with couches, game machines, and lots of cardboard cutouts (available for purchase) of current favorite characters. The staff are very friendly and helpful. Their concession stand of course offers candy and popcorn, but also ice cream and hot nachos. The fountain pop selection is broad and there are several caffeine free alternatives. The popcorn buckets offered twice a year are a great deal for frequent moviegoers - buy one and get free popcorn refills for the next five months. Check the website for promotions - when we last looked, you could get tickets to a first-run Sunday night movie for only $3 per person. Also, consider signing up for the Big Screen Movie Club to earn points towards coupons and other freebies. We'd like to see them add Monday Movies for Moms, a feature that is offered at some of their other locations.

Directions: From I-94, take exit 29, Pipestone Rd, heading north. Make an immediate left onto Mall Drive. Celebration! Cinema will be on your right, past the Best Buy. There is plenty of parking.

The Citadel Dance and Music Center

Department of Dance
91 Hinkley Street
Benton Harbor, MI 49022
Department of Music
204 Water Street
Benton Harbor, MI 49022
Department of Dance 269-925-9440
Department of Music 269-925-1099
www.citadeldmc.org

In the 1990's, Eileen Cropley and Scott Elliot bought and renovated the Old Salvation Army Building and created the Citadel Dance Center in the new Benton Harbor Arts District. In 2008, the Citadel Dance Center merged with the music education program located at the Salvation Army and expanded to become the new Citadel Dance and Music Center. The mission of the Citadel,

The Citadel Dance and Music Center (cont.)

a non-profit organization, is to develop the skills and character of individuals of every age and ethnicity through dance and music education and performance.

The Citadel offers classes in about every form of dance imaginable including movement classes for preschool age children and ballroom dancing classes for adults. Options include modern, tap, jazz, ballet, pointe, hip-hop, contemporary, Irish step-dancing, African, Zumbah, improvisational dance, belly-dancing, and Bollywood. Their teachers are excellent and they will help to place you or your child in the appropriate class whether you are an experienced dancer or a complete beginner. Serious dancers may audition for the Citadel Dancers, the performing company of the Citadel Dance and Music Center. There is also a Junior Citadel Dancers company for younger students. These dancers perform throughout the year at various venues.

The Citadel staff really cares about dance education. Eileen Cropley, the founder of the Citadel, enjoyed a career as a professional dancer and choreographer, touring and performing internationally for many years. She is well-known and well-connected in the world of dance and has attracted high-quality teachers to the Citadel. The choreography is creative and interesting and the emphasis is on dance, not on frilly costumes.

The Department of Music offers music instruction on all instruments and voice. A professionally trained faculty of 23 experienced and enthusiastic teachers offers instruction for individuals ages five through adult. Many of the instructors are active performers, members of various symphony orchestras and other musical ensembles, and artists-in-residence at area schools.

Lessons can be started at any time throughout the year. Family scheduling is accommodated and instrument assistance may be available. Kindermusic® is also offered in terms for infants through age seven who may be too young for traditional lessons.

The Citadel also runs an Instrument Petting Zoo, an outreach program allowing students the opportunity to hear, touch and try various instruments from the string, woodwind, brass and percussion families. A brief demonstration by Citadel faculty and/or students explains how the instruments produce sound and are positioned, after which participants get to experience as many as they wish. The Petting Zoo is ideal for schools, libraries, community programming, and musical venues, and all ages are welcome. There is no charge for the Zoo, but donations to the scholarship fund are appreciated.

The Citadel Dance and Music Center (cont.)

Directions: From I-94, take exit 39, Scottdale Rd/M-139N, towards Benton Harbor. Turn left on Pipestone Rd. Pipestone becomes Water St. when it crosses Main St. in downtown Benton Harbor. To get to the Dance Center, take the next left on Hinkley St.; it will be on your left. To get to the Music Center, continue on Water St. past the intersection with 6th Ave.

Dance Arts

2425 W Marquette Woods
Stevensville, MI 49127
269-429-5711
www.dancearts-sdt.com

Dance Arts is a dance studio in Stevensville that offers dance lessons for young ones in "mommy and me" type of classes (recommended age to start is 3 years old) all the way to adult ballet, tap, and even sometimes ballroom dance! They have a strong background in traditional ballet, but they also offer classes in other dance styles such as jazz, modern dance, tap, lyrical, hip-hop and more. They offer pre-dance, beginner, intermediate and advance levels of several dance styles during the school year. Classes start the second week of the shcool year and follow the Lakeshore School District calendar.

Dance Arts also offers summer lessons that usually run over the course of 6 weeks; these are a good way to get to know the studio or to get introduced to a new style of dance. They usually start sometime in June and run through July. They also offer week-long summer camps, which feature daily lessons with a theme that is age and experience appropriate. There are also other performing groups for experienced dancers linked to Dance Arts: The Studio Dance Theatre (SDT) and City Kids. SDT usually puts on a Christmas or Spring show and City Kids perform for local organizations and festivals.

The best way to get information is to call the studio and leave a message, or check out their informative website. If you leave your address, they will send you a brochure with all the information you need. Rhonda Rabbers is the owner and Director of Dance and is known as Miss Rhonda. She teaches most of the beginner levels of most dances and is always at the studio when it is open, which is usually weekdays after 4 pm. There is a little store at the studio where you can buy all equipment you need at a reasonable cost.

Directions: From I-94, take exit 23, Red Arrow Highway, going south. Take the first left onto St. Joseph Ave., then an immediate left onto W. Marquette Woods Rd. Dance Arts Studio will be on your left.

Howard Performing Arts Center

Berrien Springs, MI 49104
269-471-3560
www.howard.andrews.edu

Season runs from September - late April
Box office: Monday - Thursday 1:30 pm - 5:30 pm, Friday 1 pm - 3 pm

The Howard Performing Arts Center was designed primarily for the performance of classical music at Andrews University. The center was made possible by the university's most generous gift ever. The donation was given by John and Dede Howard, lovers of the arts and originally from Saint Joseph. The Howard Center is an exceptional arts venue that has hosted world-class performers from the international classical circuit since its opening, such as the South African group Soweto Gospel Choir, jazz vocalist Sophie Milman, Bobby McFerrin, or the Vienna Boys Choir. There is also an annual Christian Artist Series bringing artists from Point of Grace to Fernando Ortega, Avalon and Rachel Lampa.

The building sits on a prominent campus site at the end of the campus' main entry road, and faces Pioneer Memorial Church. Expert acousticians fitted the building with adjustable devices to deliver the best sound for different events, be they orchestral, sung, or spoken. It is said that from the back row of the balcony, you can hear a pin drop in the middle of the stage. The Howard Center and its seating were designed to enhance every patron's experience. There are no bad seats.

This is a fantastic resource for the campus, the local communities, and the region. It is also home of the WAUS classical radio station (90.7 FM). Additionally, the sweeping glassed large entry space serves many events like banquets and receptions. While on campus, be sure to take a peaceful walk around the beautifully groomed arboretum landscape.

Directions: From I-94, take exit 28, M-139/Old U.S. 31, southeast 8 miles to Berrien Springs. Andrews will be on the left.

Loma Theater

221 North Paw Paw Street
Coloma, MI 49038
269-468-5662
www.mooretheatres.com

You'll find this movie theater, full of charm and character, on Coloma's main street. Although the curtains and big chandeliers are gone, you will still get a feel for what this theater used to be like in its prime. The original theater has been divided into four individual small showing rooms, so there are three or four different options to watch a current movie in a cozy environment for a very reasonable price.

The chairs are not the most comfortable, but they throw in a pop and popcorn with every ticket if you get one of their buckets. Matinee shows (before 6 PM) are cheaper than evening shows. On Monday nights, if you buy two tickets you get the matinee price.

Directions: From I-94, take exit 39 toward Millburg/Coloma. Continue on Friday Road, which turns onto S. Chruch St., and then into N Paw Paw St. The Loma Theater will be on your right. There is a dirt parking lot adjacent to the building.

Mendel Center at Lake Michigan College

2755 E Napier Avenue
Benton Harbor, MI 49022
269-927-1221
www.lmcmainstage.org

Box Office open daily 10 am - 2 pm

The Mendel Center is a wonderful venue for culture and entertainment in our area. It has a main stage and several little theaters in its complex, offering performances of all kinds. You can enjoy theater, music, dance, film series, single performers like magicians or stand-up comedians and more. Performances for families and children are offered on Saturday or Sunday afternoons. Take advantage of pre-concert conversations or receptions in the adjacent Upton Hall. You can even be a volunteer and serve as an usher and see the performances while you work!

Mendel Center at Lake Michigan College (cont.)

Subscription possibilities include series or single tickets. Tickets can be purchased online or in person at the box office. Depending on how many tickets you are purchasing, sometimes a trip to the Mendel box office is worth the extra time. Parking is always abundant in the two parking lots surrounding the building. And the best part, there is no bad seat or obstructed view in the house. Even with its nearly 1,000 seats, every seat is a great seat!

Directions: From I-94, take exit 30 and turn east on Napier. There will be a large sign for the Mendel Center; turn left to enter Mendel Center parking lot.

Music in the Park

Dewey Cannon Park
14 E. Maple Street
Three Oaks, MI 49128
(Behind the Vickers Theatre)
www.harborarts.com

Saturdays throughout the summer at 7 pm
Free admission (donations welcome)

Harbor Arts produces this outdoor summer concert series at Dewey Cannon Park in Three Oaks, Michigan. The evening is always an interesting and fun mix of entertainment that is enjoyable to adults and kids alike. Past performances have incuded classical, rock, jazz, folk, reggae and other musical genres. In addition to the musical performances, the series has hosted puppet shows, poetry, Shakespeare, and silent films. Check the Harbor Arts website for a schedule of events or just stop by on a Saturday evening and enjoy the show. The performances typically last for approximately two hours. There is ample parking adjacent to the park as well as the surrounding streets.

The enviroment is very child-friendly, with plenty of room for kids to play and make new friends. Limited seating is available at the park's pavilion; however, the evening is best enjoyed from the comfort of your lawn chair or blanket with a picnic basket of your favorite refreshments. Arrive early or fashionably late, there is always plenty of space available. Don't feel like packing refreshments? There is a pizza parlor and an ice cream shop within steps of the park. No refreshments are sold on site. There is a public portable restroom located on the park grounds.

Music in the Park (cont.)

Dewey Cannon Park is not an overly-wooded area and it is located in the center of a small town. As such, insects are not usually a problem. Nonetheless, the perfomances are outdoors, so you might wish to be prepared with bug repellent.

On the third Saturday of each summer month the art galleries and select other local businesses of Three Oaks host a gallery walk with extended hours until 11 pm. At the conclusion of the evening's event at the park, enjoy a leisurely stroll through downtown to experience more music, artist demonstrations and receptions at many of the galleries.

Directions: From I-94 take exit 12. Turn left on Sawyer Road. Take third left on Three Oaks Road. Continue onto Elm Street. Turn left on Maple. Dewey Cannon Park will be on the right.

The Southwest Michigan Symphony Orchestra (SMSO)

513 Ship Street
St. Joseph, MI 49085
269-982-4030
www.smso.org

It is extremely unusual for a small community to have a professional symphony, let alone one as fabulous as the SMSO, yet the SMSO has been bringing great music to the area since 1951. Its regular season runs from September to May. The SMSO holds its concerts on the Mendel Mainstage at Lake Michigan College. These concerts provide a wide variety of programming, including pops, classical, opera, and guest artists ranging from classic Motown groups to blues vocalists to classical soloists. The SMSO also has an AroundTown Series. This is a presenting series where the SMSO brings in solists and small ensembles to perform at various venues in the community. Past venues have included the Livery in Benton Harbor, The Krasl Art Center in St. Joseph, and the Heritage Center in St. Joseph, among others.

From June through August the SMSO offers The Water's Edge Summer Music Festival, which features a series of concerts held at various beachfront venues, including the Shadowland Pavilion at Silver Beach in St. Joseph, and the Pavilion at Jean Klock Park in Benton Harbor. These concerts are a great way to spend a family evening. The venues are all beautiful and families can spend a

The Southwest Michigan Symphony Orchestra (cont.)

day at the beach and then walk straight to the concert and watch the sun set over the water as they enjoy the music. Food is always available, and many venues also offer beer and wine. Most patrons bring a beach towel or a portable chair to sit on. All venues have either bath houses or porta-potties. At the beach concerts, the SMSO performs many different styles of music including jazz, Broadway, and classical. Great guests artists also grace the stage with the orchestra. Every season brings new performances and guest artists and the SMSO runs about six concerts each summer. The beach concerts are very casual, family friendly, affordable, and enjoyable!

The Tin Shop Theatre

Corner of Days Ave. and Roe St.
Buchanan, MI 49107
269-695-6464
www.tinshoptheatre.org

Open May 21 – October 3
Shows: Friday & Saturday 7 pm – 10 pm and Sunday 4 pm – 8 pm
Box Office: Wednesday - Saturday 6 pm - 7:30 pm

The Tin Shop was built in 1865-66 by a Buchanan merchant, and has been used for many different purposes over the decades, including a furniture factory, hospital, and lumberyard. In 1984, it was repurposed yet again into the Tin Shop Theatre. This is a community endeavor, run entirely by volunteers, that puts on five different productions a year for everyone to enjoy. They offer two programs of sepcial interest to children. The first is the annual workshop, generally held during the first part of June. This is a chance for kids to get their first stage experience, which will prepare them for auditions both at the Tin Shop Theatre and elsewhere. The second item on their calendar is the children's production. While most of their shows are family-friendly, they make sure to stage one each year geared specially towards young audiences. They announce the dates of all their productions on their website.

The theater itself is intimate, seating only 74 people. The stage is raised and the seats are comfortable. There are no obstructed view seats, and in fact even the backmost rows aren't more than twenty feet from the performers. Each production usually has seven shows; on average, they last two hours, including a fifteen minute intermission. During intermission, you can buy cans of pop in the lobby; sometimes there are baked goods, but not always. If your children

The Tin Shop Theatre (cont.)

will need a snack, it's best to pack your own. On nice evenings, people stroll next door to McCoy Pond Park to get a little fresh air.

A season ticket for all events is only $32.00; adult tickets $10.00; students (ages 13-19) $9.00; children (12 & under) $5.00; senior citizen (65 or older) $9.00. Please ask for information on audience suitability before reserving your seat. The children's production usually sells out, so buy your tickets a week in advance. Tickets are purchased by calling the box office; you can leave a message if you reach them outside of operating hours.

Directions: From US-31, take exit 7, Walton Rd, heading southwest. Walton Rd becomes River St. Make a left onto Red Bud Trail. After crossing Front St in downtown Buchanan, make a right on Central Ct, then an immediate left on Days Ave. The Tin Shop Theatre will be only yards away.

Twin City Players

600 W. Glenlord Avenue
St. Joseph MI 49085
269-429-0400
www.twincityplayers.org

October - June; check website for showtimes

Older kids will enjoy the opportunity to watch or participate in the plays put on at the Twin City Players. Formed in the 1930's, the theater group prides itself on being all-inclusive. Cast and crew are all volunteers, and no experience is needed. Their season runs from October through June; five shows are staged each season. Musicals, which are popular with school groups, are usually the last show of the season. In the summertime, they run theater workshops for kids.

The schedule of shows is posted on the website, along with times for auditions and rehearsals. Tickets can be purchased by calling the box office and giving them your credit card information. Adult tickets are $12, students ages 12-18 are $11, and children under 12 are $5. Group discounts are also available.

Auditions are open and no experience is necessary, although that certain "stage presence" always helps. Many high school students participate as both cast and crew. The Fall 2009 show was crewed entirely by high school students! The

Twin City Players (cont.)

Players emphasize that they treat everyone as equals and welcome participation from all. Many volunteers return year after year and participate with their families.

A yearly fundraiser for the Twin City Players is the annual Halloween costume sale, which runs for several weekends in mid-October. The costumiers thin their wardrobe department and assemble costumes that are fully accessorized. They also accept donations of costumes throughout the year, and shop garage sales to provide the best selection. Sizes range from infant through plus-sized. If you have a specific request, the costumiers will mix and match from what's available to provide the look you want. Prices range from $5-$15 for kids and $20-$25 for adults, and include accessories. Looking through the racks at the 2009 sale, there were options ranging from vampires to Renaissance royalty to 1930's gangsters. Twin City Players is always accepting costume donations and is a great place to recycle outgrown Halloween costumes, bridesmaids dresses, and other articles of clothing.

Directions: From I-94, take exit 27, heading south. Make an almost immediate right onto Hollywood Rd. Turn right on Glenlord Rd. Twin City Players will be on your left.

Vickers Theatre

6 N Elm St
Three Oaks, MI 49128
269 756-3522
www.vickerstheatre.com

Originally built as a livery to service the nearby train station in the village of Three Oaks, Vickers Theatre has changed hands many times since the livery was converted to a theater in 1911. Currently, independent and foreign films run throughout the year. In addition to film, the theatre is home to other art forms including live theatre, music events as well as performance art and poetry readings. Held in August, the Vickers Theatre's Outdoor Film Event, the "Sound of Silents Film Festival", has become an annual summer pilgrimage for many.

The theater also supports regional filmmakers through collaborative programs with organizations such as Mid America Filmmakers. The theater's gallery

Vickers Theatre (cont.)

space features Midwestern artists and is open to the public before and between shows.

Directions: From I-94, exit 12 toward Sawyer, and make a left at Sawyer Rd. Take the third left onto 3 Oaks Rd, and continue on to N. Elm St. The theater will be on your left.

Wonderland Cinema

402 N Front St
Niles, MI 49120
269-683-1112
www.wonderlandcinema.mooretheatres.com

Wonderland Cinema is six-screen movie theater showing current releases at great prices. Concession prices are very reasonable, making this one of the most budget-friendly family outing spots in Berrien County. The hip little Wonderland Cafe is located within the cinema, which offers a variety of sandwiches and chips for $3.25. The Cafe includes a fireplace surrounded by four cozy armchairs and the decor may be described as casual contemporary. Parking is limited in the cinema's lot, but there is ample parking available in nearby municipal lots located within Riverfront Park and downtown Niles at the intersection of Sycamore and Second streets.

The super deal is free popcorn every day before noon through the popular BBOB - "Bring Back our Bucket" offer. A plastic bucket sells for $2.00. Free popcorn refills are also available Monday through Thursdays after 12 pm. All ticket prices are well below the big chains, and Mondays offer additional deals.

Directions: From US-31 take exit 7, Walton Road, east to M-139 (Old 31), and travel south 4 miles towards Niles. Wonderland Cinema will be on the west side of the road just beyond the Niles Skate Park.

NOTES:

INTRODUCTION

History comes alive at these sites. We love the chance to walk in the footsteps of early explorers, hunker down in the kitchen of a log cabin, or check out the toys of our great-grandparents. Museums also offer valuable historical insights, but these attractions, with some prepared imagination, give you a whole new perspective. Enjoy the explorations!

Allouez Park

Bond and Fort Streets
Niles, MI 49120

Allouez Park marks the grave of Father Jean Claude Allouez, who was a French Jesuit missionary in Canada and the American Midwest. Father Allouez established the first mission about 1670 in the Niles area, and is said to have instructed more than 100,000 Native Americans and to have baptized more than 10,000. A large stone cross marking his burial site is located at the top of a bluff along the Saint Joseph River, which is accessible by a series of weather-worn steps. The site is on the east side of Bond Street (unpaved road) just north of Fort Street. There is no dedicated parking, but visitors may park along the street. Allouez Park is directly across the street from Fort St. Joseph Park; together, the two offer a chance to explore some of Niles' earliest history.

Directions: From US-31, take exit 3, US-12/Pulaski Highway, heading east towards Sturgis. Travel three miles, then turn left on Bond St. Allouez Park will be one mile ahead.

Fort St. Joseph Archaeological Open House

Intersection of Fort and Bond Streets
Niles, MI
269-683-4700 ext 212
www.wmich.edu/fortstjoseph

One weekend a year; check website for date

The Fort St. Joseph Archaeological Project was initiated in 1998 by Western Michigan University archaeologists, in partnership with the city of Niles. The project is an effort to unearth the history of Fort St. Joseph, which served as a Jesuit mission, a fur trade post, and a garrison, and was occupied from 1691

Fort St. Joseph Archaeological Open House (cont.)

to 1781 by the French, and then by the British. In 2004 the Fort St. Joseph Archaeology Open House was developed as a public education initiative. Children will particularly enjoy the history scavenger hunt that allows them to search for clues to compile a booklet. Past years have also included history reenactors, lectures on the history of the fort, and open-air exhibits of the artifacts found there. The open house is free of charge.

WMU also runs a week-long archaeology camp for junior high students; budding Indiana Joneses can download an application on the website.

Directions: From US-31, take exit 3, Pulaski Hwy/US-12 E towards Niles. Make a left on Bond St. The intersection with Fort St. is about one mile up Bond St.

History Center at Court Square

313 N. Cass Street
Berrien Springs, Michigan 49103
269-471-1202
www.berrienhistory.org

June - August: Monday - Saturday 10 am - 5 pm
September - May: Monday - Friday 10 am - 5 pm

The History Center at Court Square is a striking collection of old buildings, easily visible as you drive down Cass Street into Berrien Springs. Pull into the parking lot on Union Street between the History Center and the Berrien Springs library. Follow the path past the Greek Revival courthouse to the Sheriff's Residence. This brick two-story house was built in 1870. It now houses the museum offices, and it is here that you can pick up a free self-guided walking tour pamphlet. When you enter the house, on the right you'll be able to peek into the reconstructed Sheriff's office. A plaque challenges future historians with some questions that remain unanswered today. The left side of the house holds the museum shop and offices. There is an outstanding collection of books on local history, and kids will find coloring books and paper doll collections from various historical eras.

Once you have your brochure, step back into the square to see the other buildings here. Directly to the left of the Sheriff's Residence is the Jail Plaza.

History Center at Court Square (cont.)

While the orginal jail no longer stands, there is an excellent display that gives you a good sense of the unusual architecture that was employed. The cells radiated around a central core, and cement walls mark out two of the remarkably small cells. Read the historical marker to learn about the Jailbreak of 1883. To the right of the Sheriff's Residence is Bennet's Forge. This is a recreation, originally constructed in the 1930's, that serves as an example of what was a very important part of the local economy. The forge contains an anvil, blacksmith's tools, and examples of iron work. It is a working forge one day of the year, on Pioneer Day in May, but only open to school groups of third and fourth graders.

Retrace your steps to the Courthouse, the jewel of this collection of buildings. Built in 1839, the upper floor courtroom has been restored to appear much as it did when the building was first constructed. The high ceilings and simple wood furnishings still contribute a solemn hush, and it easy to let your imagination wander back 150 years. The courthouse is used for plays, weddings, and other community functions. Downstairs, a small museum covers the span of Berrien County from prehistoric times through the 1950's. Highlights include photographs of Saint Joseph and Benton Harbor over the past seventy years. There is a charming display from the Marxochime Colony, which created unusual and futuristic-looking instruments and moved from Chicago to Berrien County in 1927. The instruments were sold by door-to-door salesmen until the company closed in the 1970's. Another notable exhibit features a wall map of Berrien, Cass and Van Buren counties from the 1860's. Incredibly detailed, each township is broken into farm plats, still clearly labelled with each family's name.

The last building open to the public is the Murdock Log House. This house was actually constructed at a different location in 1830, but moved to Court Square in 1974. Children who are reading the Little House series or other historical works will enjoy a chance to walk inside a real log cabin. The double-sided fireplace dominates the center of the room, and the low ceiling beams and logs that make up the wall are of a girth not commonly seen these days. The cabin is furnished so children and adults can clearly get a sense of what life in one of these houses may have been like.

Directions: From US-31, take exit 15, M-139, into the Village of Berrien Springs. The History Center is easily visible on the right side of the street.

Lest We Forget

www.lestweforgetusa.org

Check website for calendar of events

Lest We Forget is a group that seeks to teach the lessons of past conflicts to new generations of Americans. They work towards this goal through various educational events throughout the year. While the events change substantially year to year, the core message and enormous underlying effort remain the same. We recommend checking their website to keep up to date with their plans. The group meets the first Wednesday of each month at the Southwest Michigan Regional Airport.

The 2009 signature event was a staged reenactment of several key battles in WWII. Due to the enormous logistical effort, this will not take place annually, but we hope to see it again in the future. Watching GIs storm Jean Klock beach as if it were Normandy on D-Day is a sight not to be missed, and illustrates the efforts of the WWII soldiers in a way no movie ever could. Reenactors welcome visitors into their camps and stay in character as you talk to them, so it is a chance for kids to see a living history tableau. Lest We Forget events are well organized, with food vendors, Porta Potties, and free shuttle buses to the best viewing sites. Plan to bring chairs and cameras.

2010 brings educational displays to the St. Joseph high school football practice field. Families will have a chance to see a replica of Washington's Vietnam Wall (scaled to 80% of the original) as well as monuments to those lost on 9/11 and in the recent Afghan and Iraq conflicts. Veterans will be there to tell their stories and there will be performances of patriotic music. Kids will get a chance to enjoy a climbing wall and several simulation games. Once again, there will be food vendors and Porta Potties.

In the years to come, we look forward to more Lest We Forget programs and their valuable message.

Mary's City of David Museum

1158 East Britain Avenue
Benton Harbor, MI 49022
269-925-1601
www.maryscityofdavid.org

Saturday and Sunday 1:00 pm - 5:00 pm
June through September

This small museum (admission just $1) is a true delight, particularly when you add the historical walking tour ($4) to your visit. These tours, offered around 1:30 on Saturday or Sunday, include the print shop, carpenters' shop, garage (featuring two 1940's era tractors) and more. Whether you take part in the tour or venture out on your own, this is a great place for a family hike. Manicured trails lead past numerous fresh water springs. There are many wonders to be discovered at this unique site. Among their accomplishments, the City of David boasts the invention of the waffle cone and the auto pin set for bowling. This museum sits on a 300 acre campus of America's third oldest Christian community.

The House of David Echoes Baseball team isn't to be missed! Home games are offered throughout the spring and summer and provide spectators with an old-fashioned version of baseball you have likely never seen before. Watch for the fifth inning pepper game, which they pioneered. The team was quite famous and travelled the country extensively back in the heyday of the House of David. While the once-famous Eden Springs amusement park is largely gone, you can still get a sense of the community that has played such a large role in the history of Benton Harbor.

Directions: From I-94, take exit 28, MI-139/Scottsdale Rd, travelling north. Drive for three miles, then make a right on E Britain Ave. Mary's City of David Museum will be on your right.

The Morton House Museum

501 Territorial Road
Benton Harbor, MI 49022
269-925-7011
www.mortonhousemuseum.com

May - September
Sundays 1 pm - 4 pm or by appointment

Faded grandeur from Benton Harbor's early days is on display at the Morton House Museum. This was the private house of the Morton family, who helped found Benton Harbor and ran an important shipping company. The house was built on a hill in Benton Harbor in 1849. Today, the museum staff tries to present facets of domestic life from that era. A tour of the house takes about twenty minutes and should appeal to children ages seven and up with an interest in history.

On the first floor, you'll have a chance to tour an office equipped with old adding machines and typewriters. One machine has a numeric keyboard, but performs no calculations - its function remains a mystery. Kids enjoy the chance to look through a stereopticon, a nineteenth-century version of a Viewmaster. One bookcase holds a model of the SS Chicora, a Morton ship which sank in 1895 near Holland, and was not found until 2001. The first floor also contains the family library in its original glass-front cases. Household items, such as a desk set, a pair of glasses, and a mah jong case, are left out, just as they may have been when the family still lived here. Make sure to have kids look for the footstool whose legs are made of animal horns.

The bathrooms have the original tile work and shelves full of toiletries. The docents will explain the use of special tortoiseshell boxes, where hair taken from brushes was stored, to be used later in constructing elaborate updos. The Morton's Victrola in on display in the spacious living room, as well as the china cups used to serve tea each year to the Blossomtime queens. After touring the first floor, make your way up the staircase with its original birds eye maple paneling. The rooms upstairs have been prepared with displays of different areas of domestic life.

The dining room features place settings which seem quite elaborate to modern eyes. There's an antique telephone with a Twin Cities phone directory from 1901, and a high chair that was used by toddlers long ago. One of the bedrooms contains a spinning wheel, a butter churn, and an instrument called a

The Morton House Museum (cont.)

harmonium. Another bedroom shows how difficult it was to do laundry in those days. Kids are encouraged to lift the heavy irons and look over the scrubbing board and mangle. A small area off the hallway holds a selection of children's toys, including dolls, skates, marbles, a tea set and a rocking horse.

Morton House is in need of repairs, and is staffed by volunteers. While the admission charge is a little high ($5 for adults, $3 for kids under 15 as well as seniors,) the money is used to keep an important piece of Benton Harbor's history from slipping away.

Directions: From I-94, take exit 33, I-94 Business/E Main St. Travel 2.7 miles, then make a right on N Hull Ave. Morton House Museum will be one block ahead, on your left. Continue on N Hull Ave and make a left into the driveway, which leads to the museum's parking lot.

Pears Mill

121 South Oak Street
Buchanan, MI 49107
269-695-5525
www.cityofbuchanan.com

Open Memorial Day - Labor Day

Located in downtown Buchanan, Pears Mill is the last mill left out of thirteen that once harnessed the water flow of McCoy Creek. The water wheel is connected to the creek by a small canal, called a mill race, that was dug in the 1850's. The race provides a ten-foot drop of water, enough to turn the wheel and thus the powerful grindstones. Unfortunately, damage to the race will likely prevent the mill from grinding in 2010; there are plans to make the mill operational once more in years ahead.

In the meantime, there are still fun family activities to be had at the huge building. The mill has been carefully restored, and the exposed post beams and 12 over 12 windows are an excellent example of Italianate Greek Revival architecture. Inside, you'll find working hand-operated farm tools, which kids are welcome to try. The mill provides corn so kids can crank the corn sheller; it gets very noisy as the kernels are stripped off the cobs. The potato sorter is another popular exihibit. You can learn more about community history from

Pears Mill (cont.)

the displays of signs from bygone Buchanan businesses, and kids always enjoy the models of other mills, now gone, that ground grains for area farmers. Although the water wheel is not currently working, you are welcome to examine the wheel and gears to understand how this early but powerful technology works.

Pears Mill hosts an annual Regional History Day, where many different non-profits gather and provide educational displays. Call ahead for details. The mill also has rotating exhibits. We look forward to the planned collection of nineteenth century household tools, including an old cookstove and butter churn. Kids who are studying history of the past 150 years will enjoy a chance to see their lessons come alive.

Group tours can be arranged. There are occasional special exhibits of crafts such as blacksmithing and weaving. Admission to the mill is free, but please consider a donation to help restore the mill to working order, and support the educational efforts.

Directions: From US-31, take exit 5, Niles-Buchanan Rd, towards Buchanan. Continue as it becomes E Front St. Turn left on S Oak St. Pears Mill will be on the left. There is a free parking lot.

INTRODUCTION

Drive a race car. Shoot a hole in one. Storm the castle and capture the flag. Amusement parks let kids take on heroic tasks that have been scaled down to their size. The sense of accomplishment they experience as they tackle these challenges is wonderful to see. Brookview toddlers live by the credo "I did it myself!" as they fold their own towels and wipe down their tables. These amusement parks can allow your older children to experience that same sense of achievement as they try out new and daring deeds.

Captain Mike's Fun Park

10975 Red Arrow Highway
Bridgman, MI 49106
269-465-5747
www.captainmikesfunpark.com

Open Memorial Day - Labor Day

Captain Mike's Fun Park is located on five park-like acres off the Red Arrow Highway. Most of their main attractions are designed to be enjoyed by even the smallest children, making this a terrific family attraction. For example, they have two-seater go-karts so that kids under ten get a chance to ride on the big track - and they ride free with an adult! Even better, there's a smaller race track where young drivers, ages 5 - 10, get a chance to practice driving. A bridge and tunnel make this race course exciting for the young ones, while parents sit back and realize how soon their babies will be getting their drivers' licenses. The bumper boats also offer a two-seater option. Water cannons are mounted on the side of the pool, so bring clothes to change into once you're done.

The arcade offers skee-ball, air hockey, and other games where you can earn tickets to redeem for prizes. An eighteen hole mini-golf course includes a lighthouse and water features. There are also batting cages and the chance to shoot basketballs while jumping on a trampoline. You can purchase nachos, hot dogs and similar snacks and enjoy them at picnic tables in the open air. While there is no admission charge, you have to buy tickets to each attraction, and tokens for the arcade games. Bring money because your kids will want to try it all. It is worth the grin on your darlings' faces as they go whirling by in their tiny cars.

Directions: From I-94, take exit 16 towards Bridgman; turn right on Red Arrow Highway and travel for less than one mile. Captain Mike's Fun Park will be on your left.

Hidden Pointe Fun Park

1062 Nickerson Avenue
Benton Harbor, MI 49022
269-926-1358
www.hiddenpointe.net

Open May - October, depending on the weather
Monday - Saturday 11 am - 11 pm
Sunday noon - 11 pm

Hidden Pointe is visible from I-94 as you drive past Benton Harbor. It's worth your while to stop by for a closer look. They have a lot of really fun outdoor activities. The miniature golf course is beautifully landscaped and the greens are very well maintained. The eighteen holes are laid out in a circle around a central lighthouse. If you get a good score, you can have the staff write your name on the leaderboard for bragging rights. They have putters in a wide range of sizes, accomodating even very young players.

Local baseball and softball teams stop by for practice in the batting cages. The go-kart track with banked turns is terrific, and has lights that let you drive late into the evening. If you get hungry, you can purchase candy or Sherman's ice cream. They have some picnic tables and you are welcome to bring your own treats to enjoy. There is a small arcade room and a nifty trampoline basketball game that gives new meaning to the words "jump shot." Restrooms are available. Hidden Pointe can be booked for parties.

Directions: From I-94, take exit 28, travelling north on M-139. Make a right on Nickerson and travel 0.3 miles. Hidden Pointe Fun Park will be on your right.

Kelley's Bowl

2705 Cleveland Ave.
St. Joseph, MI 49085
269-983-3034
www.frosproshop.com

Monday, Wednesday, Thursday and Sunday: noon - 11 pm
Tuesday: noon - 10 pm
Friday and Saturday: noon - midnight
Hours somewhat shorter June - August; call ahead to confirm

Kelley's Bowl (cont.)

Kelly's Bowl is close enough to St. Joseph High School to make it a great after-school meeting place, especially when it is cold. It has all of the things you would expect from a neighborhood bowling alley - a pro-shop, an arcade, vending machines, and of course 30 lanes with auto score and kid bumpers. Kelley's offers "Family Time" on Saturdays and Sundays from noon - 5 pm. The price is $7.00 and it includes two games and shoes. There is also a birthday party option complete with kid friendly program (balloons, pizza, decorations, and shoes) for $12.00 per child (minimum 8 kids). They have rates for grown-up parties and events as well. League night is Monday, and is the only day of the week where reservations are not accepted. Friday and Saturday are Cosmic Bowling with glow-in-the-dark balls and pins from 9 pm - midnight. Check the website for rotating specials on games and rentals.

There are two full service bars if you are over 21, but one bar is usually reserved for events. The Snack Bar has hot food and soft drinks. We look forward to the statewide ban on indoor smoking; until then, the weekend Family Time is smoke-free.

Directions: From I-94, take exit 27, Niles Road, towards St. Joseph. Make a right on Hilltop and another right on Cleveland. Kelley's Bowl will be on your left.

Silver Beach Carousel

333 Broad Street
St. Joseph, MI 49085
269-982-8500
www.silverbeachcarousel.com

Thursday - Saturday 10 am - 5 pm
Sunday noon - 5 pm

The Silver Beach Carousel Society worked for years to bring back a carousel to Saint Joseph, and now we all can benefit from their hard work. The carousel has been delighting children and families since January 2010. It is housed in a soaring glass-fronted building with a roof that echoes a big-top circus tent. The forty-eight figures, all hand carved, are truly a delight. Children can choose among animals such as a panda, a praying mantis, a dinosaur and a dolphin, among any others. The high school mascots from Saint Joseph, Stevensville

Silver Beach Carousel (cont.)

and Benton Harbor are represented with pride. Each figure is a work of art with delightful details such as a butterfly perched on the nose of a horse, or a small lamb or kitten hitching a ride on the saddle. One of the two chariots is handicap-accessible. There are wooden rocking chairs set around the perimeter to sit in as you pick out the animal for your next ride. The rounding boards are decorated with pictures of local history, and overall the carousel is stunning. Rides are $2 per person; kids under 42 inches tall ride free, but must have a paying adult accompany them. Prices are better if you purchase multiple tokens. There are token machines inside the carousel room that take bills from $1 to $20, but they do not give change. The small room just behind the band organ has a detailed model of the old Silver Beach amusement park, as well as some funhouse mirrors and old photographs of Silver Beach.

Slackers Family Fun Center

Orchards Mall, Entrance #3
1800 Pipestone Road
Benton Harbor, MI 49022
269-325-7525

Monday - Thursday noon - 9 pm
Friday and Saturday 10 am - 11 pm
Sunday 11 am - 6 pm

Slackers is an indoor entertainment center that advertises fun for kids ages 2 to 97. From a younger kid's perspective, Slackers is a no-brainer because youngsters love the arcade games and laser tag. But it's also common to see parents joining the fun. For parents who choose not to partake in the games, Slackers is still a plus because it works for any day of the week, and especially for rainy days. While the kids play, parents can enjoy shopping in the mall or hang out in the Slackers lobby. The lobby is an appreciably quiet space, comfortable enough to enjoy a conversation and watch mall shoppers pass by.

The arcade games area is family-friendly and not overwhelmingly shoot 'em up nor as raunchy as some arcades. All machines operate with tokens purchased at the front counter. Depending on how skillful or lucky you are, you will receive tickets that may be redeemed for prizes at the ticket redemption counter. The prizes consist of candies, small toys and trinkets.

Slackers Family Fun Center (cont.)

The laser tag game works like this: A Slackers employee gathers the players in a room to introduce the rules, teams are formed (identified by different colored electronic lighted vests and headphone sets), or the players agree to play as individuals. Attached to each vest is a gun-shaped laser shooting device. The teams are placed in a darkened maze-like environment to "shoot" at each other. Because the game is electronic, all shots are recorded for later review. After each round (about 15 minutes) the players gather in the lobby to see their individual and team scores. Don't worry, if you don't know how to play, you can watch the activity from monitors in the lobby, and instructors are on hand to answer questions.

Laser tag is fun for individuals, but especially so for groups of friends, and it's perfect for a birthday party. Tag prices vary; each game costs $6 to play, and is about 15 minutes long. Sometimes Slackers has specials on laser tag, where you can generally play as long as you want for $15.

Directions: From I-94, take exit 29, Pipestone Rd. Go about 1/2 mile on Pipestone; Orchards Mall is on the left. Slackers is closest to Entrance 3.

Surfari Joe's

8258 Arnt Boulevard
Watervliet, MI 49808
269-463-7946
www.surfarijoes.com

Friday (and Thursday in the summer):
3:15 pm - 6:30 pm
6:45 pm - 10 pm
Saturday: 8:00 am - 10:30 am
11:45 am - 3 pm
3:15 pm - 6:30 pm
6:45 pm - 10 pm
Sunday: 8:00 am - 11 am

The Michigan winters, we all know, can get pretty long. If a beach getaway isn't an option, a day trip to Surfari Joe's might do the trick. Surfari Joe's is part of the Ramada Inn in Watervliet. If you're not a guest of the hotel, you can purchase a day pass to use this cool indoor water park. The building is is easy to spot from I-94, thanks to the colorful waterslides twisting down the side of the building. A day at Surfari Joe's is broken up into sessions as noted above.

Surfari Joe's (cont.)

Tickets are $10 per person per session, and $20 for the whole day. Park at the far end of the Ramada parking lot - the door to Surfari Joe's opens onto the lot. The ticket office is inside, to your right.

Your kids will get excited the minute they walk in the building. Pygmy Pond is only six inches deep, and is dominated by a large climbing structure with slides and nets. Kids can control the water cannons and fountains bubble up from the platform. The most exciting feature happens on average every five minutes. A bell starts to clang, giving people time to get into - or out of - the way. Then a giant bucket, shaped like an elephant head and holding 85 gallons of water, overturns. The water crashes off the roof of the climbing tower and makes a huge splash into the pond. The roof and bucket are strategically placed so that nobody gets hit with too forceful a splash.

The water slides are tremendous fun, and new rules at Surfari Joe's open them up to younger children. The yellow slide is ridden with tubes, and they now have double tubes so that kids under 48" tall can ride down with an adult. The blue slide remains reserved for those over the height limit and doesn't use a tube. You climb three flights of stairs to get to the slide platform, where a lifeguard keeps order and helps you down the slide. The slide is really fast and fun and very easy to ride; no steering or readjustments required. You splash down into a pool, where you can climb out and start again. Another lifeguard is on duty to help younger children off their tubes and onto the pool deck. There is sometimes a short wait for a double tube, but the line moves quite quickly.

Even younger children who dislike the splashing in Pygmy Pond will enjoy paddling around in the quieter sections of the pool. Swim diapers are allowed throughout the park, and the office has a supply, but we suggest bringing your own if you can. Infant sized inner tubes with a solid bottom keep young ones secure. The quiet pool is connected to the River Run, a twisting channel with a rapid current that is strong enough to pull adults along with minimal effort. Using the inner tubes, you can ride in a circuit through River Run again and again. Finally, there's a hot tub in the corner, under the bar, with a waterfall feature. The pool temperature is 83 degrees, while the hot tub is set at 100.

The bathroom facilities are clean and well-kept, but some benches and more private changing areas would be a welcome addition. Towels are provided at the office, but they are small and skimpy, so we recommend bringing your own. There are shelves and bins to keep your clothes, but no lockers - valuables should be stored in the car outside.

Surfari Joe's (cont.)

The Water Hole is a full bar overlooking the pool. A party room is available for rental at $100/hr, plus food, beverage, and water park tickets. Lifeguards are on duty and are friendly and helpful.

Directions: I-94 to Exit 41, go north towards Watervliet. Arnt Boulevard is on your immediate right; the Ramada Inn and Surfari Joe's are at the end of the road on your right. The park is visible from I-94.

NOTES:

INTRODUCTION

Berrien County is rich in community celebrations. These festivals and parades commemorate local events, such as a peach harvest, or a common interest, such as classic cars. They can expand our horizons with brand-new art and music, or they can be part of traditions over a century old. Whatever the reason, these special times bring us all together. Brookview families enjoy the school's community celebrations, including movie nights, Slow Snack canning parties, and Mardi Gras. We're also likely to be found at all of the events described in this chapter. Who doesn't love a parade?

Artoberfest

The Benton Harbor Arts District
Benton Harbor, MI 49022
www.newterritoryarts.org

Third weekend in September

Artoberfest is held annually in the fall and is a celebration of local art and music. The event, held in the Benton Harbor Arts District, is a great way to spend some time listening to a wide assortment of live music, meeting local artists who have their work displayed and for sale, and enjoying locally brewed beers from the Livery, a local brew-pub.

The event always has a relaxed atmosphere and is very child-friendly. The Benton Harbor Arts District is the home of many artists' studios and most are open during the event. The artists are more than happy to show off their studios and explain their crafts.

Although there are porta-potties available, bathrooms in some of the studios are open to the public and are a better option for families with young children.

Directions: From I-94, take exit 29, Pipestone Road, towards Benton Harbor. Turn right on Main Street in downtown Benton Harbor, then take a right on Fifth Street. There are several parking lots in the area, as well as street parking.

Barodafest

Baroda, MI 49101
269-422-1779
www.barodavillage.org

Saturday after Labor Day, 7 am - 11 pm

The Village of Baroda holds an annual festival the Saturday after Labor Day. This is a small town with a huge spirit for fun! Barodafest is a full day of family activities. Start the day off right at the pancake breakfast. There is a 5K run/walk to raise awareness for organ donation. Kids enjoy the car and tractor shows. The festival includes a small parade, and the winner of the Miss Baroda pageant appears with her court. Bakers can compete in the pie baking contest or the kids' cookie baking contest. Special events in the past have included a 3 on 3 basketball tournament and a House of David old-fashioned baseball game. Vendors set up booths selling arts and crafts as well as tasty festival food. This is a homey event that winds down with evening music and karaoke under the stars.

Directions: From I-94, take exit 16. Follow Red Arrow Highway east toward Bridgman. Turn right at Lake St and go four miles to the Cleveland Ave stop sign. Turn left on Cleveland Ave and take the next right on Church St (1st street to right). Parking is located off Third & Second Sts in the Legion Field.

Berrien County Youth Fair

9122 Old US-31 Hwy
Berrien Springs, MI 49103
269-473-4251
www.bcyf.org

One week in August annually

The Berrien County Youth Fair is a premier attraction in Berrien County. Our families love the fair's focus on the work of youths ages 5 - 20. Participation as an exhibitor is free, rewarding, and highly recommended. Check out the fair's website, where the exhibitor handbook can be downloaded in late spring. You can also browse a copy at any public library. Inside, you'll find a huge range of categories in which kids can compete. Kids can enter drawings, painting, original stories, Lego and Erector Set constructions, wildflower arrangements,

Berrien County Youth Fair (cont.)

baked goods, insect collections and much more. This is also an agricultural fair, so categories include home-grown fruits, vegetables and livestock. Exhibitors must register by August 1st, then turn in their projects the Sunday before the fair. Judging takes place by Monday night, and you can pick up your exhibit at the end of the fair. Exhibitors need not be present for judging. Every entry receives a grade from the judges, and a check for a token amount (usually $1-3) is given based on the grade. Kids are thrilled to have their work exhibited and rewarded. Even better, exhibitors receive free admission to the fair all week long! This focus on youth work is what really makes the Berrien County Youth Fair a fantastic event for families. Most of the entries are proudly completed without parental "help."

When visiting the fair, you can purchase tickets in advance or at the gate. If you're attending on more than one day, the week-long pass is a good bargain. The carnival rides start Monday afternoon and are present throughout the week. There are usually "wristband" days with unlimited rides for a set fee, as well as other promotions. There are rides appropriate for ages from preschooler to teen, including classics like "The Octopus" and kiddie trains and cars. Fair food includes fried staples such as corn dogs and elephant ears. We recommend checking out some of the many booths set up by churches and local civic groups - this is where you can purchase homestyle cooked fare that is a little healthier. During the day, if you need a break from the sun, stroll the main exhibit hall, which is enclosed. Families with young children recommend taking a wagon along to prevent tired feet. Unless it has been a wet summer, bugs usually are not a problem at the fair. If you're planning to spend lots of time there at dusk, or near the livestock exhibits, some bug spray may come in handy.

The fair also includes some grandstand events, usually live music acts, tractor pulls, and a demolition derby. These require separate tickets. The acts are announced well in advance and can sell out quickly.

We have included directions to the back entrance of the fair. This is usually a quicker route and the parking lot puts you close to the exhibition hall.

Directions: Traveling towards Berrien Springs on M-139, take a right onto Redbud Trail, just before the overpass over US-31. At the first stop sign, take a left on E. Shawnee Rd. The back entrance to the fair will be on your left.

Blossomtime Parade

Downtown St. Joseph and Benton Harbor
www.blossomtimefestival.org

Second Saturday in May

There is a lot of wonderful local history tied up in the Blossomtime Festival, which will celebrate its 105th anniversary in 2011. The highlight of the festival is the Grand Floral Parade, which draws spectators from all over the Midwest. The parade route starts on Main Street in downtown St. Joseph and travels over the bridge into Benton Harbor. People start putting out chairs and blankets early in the morning. Check out the Herald Palladium (www.heraldpalladium.com) for the route and times. The west side of Main Street tends to be less crowded, but you must get across the street well before the parade start time in order to avoid being cut off. The east side of the street has easier access to parking in the surrounding neighborhoods. The bands and floats are all prepared on the side streets, so expect to park your car and walk. It's fun for smaller kids to get a chance to see the elaborately decorated vehicles up close. The high school kids who ride on the floats as winners from the Blossomtime Pageants are often happy to take pictures and may even let your little ones up on the float for a minute.

The west side (closest to the lake) of Main Street is closed starting several hours before the parade, which opens up prime real estate for seating. Football players from the local high schools typically sell programs so you can tell which floats are coming up. For more than forty years, the parade has started with the amazing Indianapolis Metropolitan Police Motorcycle Drill Team. They weave in and out, ride their motorcycles standing up, and make sure to go back and forth several times so that everyone gets a great view. The St. Joseph and Benton Harbor High School bands alternate positions each year as the first and last bands of the parade. In between, you'll see marching bands from all over Berrien County. Other parade favorites include equestrian teams, antique tractors, clown cars and more. The floats are very elaborate and each presents the community's pageant winners.

The parade lasts about two hours. The weather is variable and it is best to dress in layers. Food and drinks can be purchased from vendors that set up along the parade route. There are porta-potties set up on both sides of the parade route.

Niles Bluegrass Festival

Niles Riverfront Park
On the corner of Main and Front Sts.
Niles, MI 49120
www.nilesbluegrass.com

Yearly, in early June

2010 will be the 8th year for the Niles Bluegrass Festival. It is a great 4-day family event in the beautiful Riverfront Park on the banks of the St. Joe River in downtown Niles. Local and national touring acts provide one of the best weekends of music in the Midwest. Both traditional and non-traditional acts perform on 2 stages. If you play, make sure to bring your guitar. There are workshops for musicians, a picker's tent, and players at all levels participate in jam sessions on stage with some of the bands. Browse the arts and crafts vendor booths; have lunch or dinner in the open air from some of the many food booths. Strawberry shortcake is a particular specialty. People travel from all over to attend the festival, and many set up campers and tents in Riverfront Park. You can also enjoy a great selection of amusement rides for young and old. There are special kids' activities such as soap carving. This is a free festival and a terrific value for families.

Directions: From US-31, take exit 5, Niles/Buchanan Rd, towards Niles. The road becomes Grant St as you enter town. Make a left on Lincoln Ave, then a right onto Main St. Cross over the St. Joseph River. Front St will be at your immediate left.

Blues, Brews and BBQ Festival

Howard Bandshell
Port Street
St. Joseph, MI 49085
www.sjtoday.org

One Saturday in mid-September, noon - 6 pm

Celebrate one final summer weekend in downtown St. Joseph at the Blues, Brews and BBQs Festival. This is a relatively new addition to the St. Joseph calendar, and it's still working to find its groove. There is live music at the

Blues, Brews and BBQ Festival (cont.)

Howard bandshell, with two or three musicians contributing sets. Take a seat on the benches to listen, or wander around Port Street and enjoy the music as background atmosphere. Different restaurants have set up booths in the past, including Port 412, Charlie's Piggin 'n' Grinnin', and Larks. They have run out of food before the end of the festival, so make sure to get there closer to lunch time in order to be able to try it all. At the 2009 Festival, the Round Barn winery offered two of their brews.

Teams of up to four players register in advance for the Xtreme Bean Bag Tournament. This is a local sport that also goes colloquially as "Cornhole." The Official Tournament rules can be found on the St. Joe Today website and are six pages long. Essentially, you try to toss a beanbag into a hole. Each team pays a $25 reigstration fee and must sign up in advance; team members receive a T-shirt.

The festival is not heavily attended, so parking and maneuvering should not be a problem. If the weather is nice, it's a pleasant way to spend an afternoon and sample some local restaurants you might have otherwise missed.

Directions: Port Street between Lake Boulevard and State Street is closed off for the festival; use the downtown parking lots and walk down Lake Boulevard towards the river.

Chalk the Block

Lake Bluff Park
St. Joseph, MI 49085
www.sjtoday.org

First weekend in August

Chalk the Block enters its ninth year in 2010. This is a pleasant summer festival whose highlight is the elaborate sidewalk chalk art along Lake Bluff Park. The artists work on large spaces, up to 10' by 10', to create whimsical designs and trompe l'oeil effects. Open to both amateur and professional artists, there is no charge to participate, but artists must apply in advance to be matched with a sponsor. Local merchants offer sidewalk sales, and there are musical performances at the Whitcomb and the Howard Bandshell. For the past four years, the Naschair Challenge has been an additional draw. Held on the Friday

Chalk the Block (cont.)

of the festival, crews of four propel an actual office chair down a street-length race course. Elaborate pit crew costumes and chair decorations add to the fun, and the Challenge benefits Habitat for Humanity. On Saturday, families can shop the weekly Farmer's Market, admire the chalk paintings, and participate in kids' activities at the Krasl, the library, and Curious Kids Museum.

Concours on the Bluff

Lake Bluff Park
St. Joseph, MI 49085
269-983-0742
www.krasl.org

One Saturday in August, 10 am - 4 pm; check website for details

Concours on the Bluff is a juried show of classic cars. It is a fundraiser for the Krasl Art Center, which has been hosting the event annually since 2004. Car collectors from all over the Midwest are invited to enter their cars, and the show spans almost the entire era of automotive history. Past entrants have included a French car from 1897, a Rolls Royce Silver Ghost, a 1911 Model T, and a 1953 Hudson Hornet. All of the cars are buffed and polished to a high gloss, and some of the owners dress in period costume to match their cars. They are quite knowledgeable about their vehicles and are available to answer questions. Young children need to be reminded not to touch the valuable machines. The entrance fee in 2009 was $5 per person; families with children under 16 were charged a flat $10 fee. Local restaurants offer food for sale at booths along the display grounds. Lake Bluff Park has a sidewalk suitable for pushing strollers, but some of the cars may be best approached on the lawn.

Easter Egg Hunt and Easter Bonnet Parade

Lake Bluff Park, St. Joseph
www.sjtoday.org

Date and time vary each year

The Easter Egg Hunt is an amazing thing to see. You will never again wonder if your child is incapable of cleaning up their room. Sections of Lake Bluff Park across from the Krasl Art Center are roped off . Each section is for a

Easter Egg Hunt and Easter Bonnet Parade (cont.)

different age group, and the age ranges are kept narrow to give all the kids a fair chance at getting some eggs. Inside, the ground is thickly carpeted with plastic eggs; each usually contains a small toy. When the fire engine blows the siren, the ropes are dropped and the herd of children descend on the eggs. Parents snap pictures, and the lawn is usually picked clean within thirty seconds. The two and three year olds often need a little coaxing. If you have kids of different ages, it's strongly recommended to let each participate in their own age group, so that they each have a good chance of getting some eggs. The Egg Hunt gets very crowded in years where the weather is nice, so have an adult to keep track of each child. Make sure the kids have a basket to carry their haul.

After the hunt, there is the Easter Bonnet Parade down Lake Street. This is a relatively informal affair, with no registration required and no particular marching order. Frequently, there are more marchers than spectators. It is fun to see the elaborate bonnets and matching outfits that people put together. The parade awards a prize for best bonnet at the terminus of the parade, the St. Joseph Welcome Center.

Three Oaks Flag Day Parade

Elm Street
Three Oaks, MI
www.3oaks.org

Annually; second Sunday in June at 3 pm.

The tiny village of Three Oaks claims to host the largest Flag Day parade in the country. Parade entrants include marching bands, drill teams, tractors and horses. The parade participants traditionally throw candy to the spectators. Most of the candy has been thrown before reaching the train tracks. If your kids want to get some candy be sure to be at the start of the parade route, at the north end of town on Elm Street. The parade is broadcast live on Three Oaks' own community radio station, WRHC-FM 106.7. Be sure to bring your radio and a bag for the candy!

Directions: From I-94, take exit 4A, Pulaski Highway/US-12E towards Niles. As you enter the town of Three Oaks, make a right onto Elm St. Elm St. is the parade route; Hickory St. is two blocks further and runs parallel to Elm.

Four Flags Apple Festival

Lake and 17th Streets
Niles, MI 49120
www.fourflagsapplefestival.org

Third full weekend after Labor Day
Thursday 3 pm - 10 pm
Friday 3 pm - 11 pm
Saturday 7 am - 11 pm
Sunday 7 am - 6 pm

Youth day takes place the Saturday before the festival

Niles hosts the Four Flags Apple Festival each fall, an annual event for more than thirty years. All the classic elements of an American celebration are included, and it's a lot of fun. They have a big selection of contests open to the public and broken down into different age divisions. Kids can compete at apple pie eating, apple peeling, log sawing, seed popping, and scarecrow decorating. There are also competitions for the best apple baked goods, and growers from around the state view to win the biggest apple award. The contests for the longest and most unusual beards and mustaches are a festival highlight. Even if you don't want to compete, these are designed to be great fun for the audience too. Downtown stores get in on the action, decorating their windows with hopes of being crowned the winner.

The Apple Festival hosts a full-fledged carnival with lots of rides, including a Ferris Wheel and merry-go-round. Tickets for each ride must be purchased separately, but there are $20 wristband nights on Thursday and Saturday. There's live music in the entertainment tent on Friday and Saturday night. The main event on Saturday is the Grand Parade, which winds a five mile route through downtown Niles and includes marching bands, pageant floats, and fire and rescue vehicles. Also on Saturday after dusk is the big fireworks show.

The Custom Car show is held on the Sunday of the festival, and includes live music while you get the chance to check out literally hundreds of decked-out cars. Sunday is also the day of the horseshoe tournament, where single players and teams of two and four people compete in single elimination rounds throughout the day. The craft show takes place on Saturday and Sunday and usually draws up to 200 different vendors. Per festival rules, all vendors must offer homemade products, and you can find quilts, ornaments, lawn decor and more.

Four Flags Apple Festival (cont.)

Up to 115,000 people attend the festival over the course of the four days. If that seems a little overwhelming for your family, we highly recommend Youth Day, held the preceding Saturday. This is a more laid-back celebration especially designed for families with younger children. There are trike and Big Wheel races, clowns, face painting, games, and sack races. Local elementary schools usually band together to enter the Youth Parade. Everyone who attends receives hot dogs and other treats for free. In past years, the Boy Scouts have set up rope climbing courses, and the Curious Kids' Museum has also particiapted.

Admission to the Apple Festival is free. You can park at the grounds for a $5 donation; expect to walk about 1/2 block to the start of the fair. There are Porta-Johns and handwashing stations placed throughout the fairgrounds. Up to 65 vendors sell food of all kinds, from elephant ears to Japanese food to barbecued ribs to soup in a bread bowl. They have large tents set up to let you get a break from inclement weather.

Directions: From US-31, take exit 5, Niles-Buchanan Rd, towards Niles. The road becomes Grant St as you enter the town. Turn left on N Lincoln Ave, then right onto W Main St. Make a left on N 5th St, then right on Lake St. The festival will be one mile down Lake St.

Fourth of July Celebrations

There are lots of fireworks displays to choose from. Dusk falls very late in summer in Berrien County, since we are on the westernmost edge of the Eastern Time Zone. This means that fireworks shows often have to start quite late. Parents with younger children often seek out the smaller shows to minimize meltdowns. Wherever you go, pack bug spray and a snack. Shows that take place near the lake can get cold once the sun sets, so dress in layers. There are other fireworks shows in Berrien County, but these three are some of our favorites.

Saint Joseph (July 4):
The fireworks at Saint Joseph draw big crowds. The show starts late, close to 11 pm, to allow for maximum effect. The best viewing area is at Silver Beach, and people stake out prime viewing spots well in advance. Expect crowds from the water's edge all the way back to the parking lot. The fireworks are shot off from the pier; Jean Klock park is expected to become a more popular viewing spot with the new facilities in that park. Don't expect to find downtown parking easily; we suggest parking on the east side of Main Street in the neighborhoods

Fourth of July Celebrations (cont.)

and walking to Silver Beach. Strollers will limit your mobility due to the crowds, as well as the sand. One popular strategy for locals with children is to park further south, near the Dairy Korner (1605 Lakeview Rd). Take the public access walkway over the train tracks and down to Lion's Beach. You'll have to walk uphill on the way home, but you'll miss the worst of the crowds and traffic.

People also decorate their boats and watch the fireworks from the Lake. The channel is closed after a certain time, and the Coast Guard enforces a safety zone around the pier, where the fireworks are shot from.

New Buffalo (July 4):
This fireworks show starts a little earlier, at 9:45 pm. Park in downtown New Buffalo and walk down Whittaker St. There's a small park on your right that overlooks the marina; this park is less crowded than the beach and offers a fine view, plus room for a quick getaway if your kids get too tired. Stop by Nancy's on Whittaker St, since they stay open late to sell their famous strawberry shakes. If you want the full experience, the Southwest Michigan Symphony Orchestra puts on a show of live music starting at 7 pm at the beach pavilion, but you need to purchase tickets in advance.

Baroda (July 3):
Baroda's fireworks are very accessible. They take place behind the American Legion Hall, in a field. People park their cars in the field and tailgate, or bring lawnchairs and blankets to move closer to the hall. A band starts playing several hours before dusk, and the American Legion sets up a beer tent selling beers and bratwurst. The hall address is 9214 1st St.

Glad-Peach Festival

Coloma, MI
www.colomapeachfest.com

First full weekend in August

The Glad-Peach Festival has been held annually for over forty years. It celebrates two local products, peaches and gladiolus flowers. Coloma's small size makes this festival manageable with young children, and there are lots of attractions for kids to enjoy. These include a carnival with rides, two parades, a fireworks show, and food tents featuring lots of peach specialties. In addition, there's a baking competition and an associated arts and crafts fair. Live music and dance troupes offer shows to keep the mood festive. There are several road races to enter, including 10K and 5K runs, and a 5K walk. People often sit along the race routes to cheer on the participants.

Free parking and a shuttle bus are available at Great Lakes Antiques on Ryno Road, just off Exit 39 from I-94, before you reach town. Otherwise, you can pay for parking at various spots within walking distance of the festivities. The various booths and tents are spread over four or five blocks in downtown Coloma, so bring a wagon or stroller for young children.

Directions: Coloma is located at exit 39 off I-94. Take Friday Rd. into downtown Coloma.

Krasl Art Fair

707 Lake Boulevard
St. Joseph, MI 49085
269-983-0271
www.krasl.org

Second weekend in July
Saturday, 10 am - 6 pm
Sunday 10 am - 5 pm

This juried art fair couldn't be much more family-friendly. First and foremost, save yourself a long hike and use the parking shuttles provided. Current shuttle locations are always on the website and signs are posted throughout town. The fair runs along Lake Bluff Park from the fountain all the way to the Krasl Art Center. If you're determined to see the whole show (more than 200 booths)

Krasl Art Fair (cont.)

start on the north end and use the food court and Krasl Kids Zone as motivating factors to keep young legs moving. Once you're at the fair, you'll find services for children of all ages.

The Food Court provides all types of unique food and beverage vendors. Tables and chairs are provided, although there isn't much shade in the parking lot that serves as food court. Often, you'll find live music here so you can "shake a leg with the whole family." If you need shade or a more relaxed atmosphere to enjoy your meal, the food court is located just a half block from downtown, where there are many restaurants.

Parents of young children may wish to stop at the Baby Services Tent located in the side yard of the public library. There you'll find a changing table, rocking chairs, shade, water, and a few toys for toddlers or siblings. This nursing-friendly facility is also a great place for families with children of all ages to take a break from the crowds. Dedicated volunteers maintain and restock the space. This is a better bet for diaper changes than most restaurants.

In the Krasl Art Center's yard is the Krasl Kids Zone. For a nominal donation, volunteers provide your family with a handful of simple art activiites. Sometimes your family will be adorned with fun hats or other wearables after a visit to the Kids Zone. During select years, henna artists or facepainters will rent a space at the Kids Zone. When this is the case you may find longer lines and a fee for participation. Adjacent to the Kids Zone is one of the three performing artists stages. At this stage you will find interactive programming specifically for families. Note, it is not permitted to leave your children unattended at the Krasl Kids Zone.

If you happen to have a young art aficionado in your family, give them twenty dollars and let them select their own works of art. About half of the artists commit to participating in the Children's Art Purchase Program. These artists have artwork available for children only for $10 or less. Look for the orange flags to find the CAPP artists.

We've got a few tips to make this heavily attended fair more manageable. If there is one artist you just don't want to miss, download the map prior to the fair so you can easily plan your trip. To avoid the port-a-potties, try the restrooms at the Krasl Art Center. Finally, for families with young children, you'll find the crowded artist booths and narrow walk-ways much easier to navigate with a baby carrier than a stroller. Pets are not allowed at the Krasl Art Fair.

Latin Taste and Rhythms Festival

101 Broad Street
St. Joseph, MI 49085
www.sjtoday.org

Typically held in July or August; check website for details

In the fresh outdoors at the Shadowland Pavilion, the Latin Taste & Rhythms Festival brings in crowds of both locals and tourists to enjoy the great tastes of local Latin food, with live bands bringing folkloric music from a variety of Hispanic cultures. Celebrating the Latin culture is what brings such a diverse group together. Music acts include salsa as well as merengue from the Chicago band "Hector Silveira y su Orquestra." Dancers from Benton Harbor's Citadel perform terrific Latin dances. Enjoy a meal from La Perla Produce (Mexican cuisine,) Cravings Catering (Cuban,) Kilwin's Ice Cream and more.

All proceeds from this great event are invested right back into the local community in support of families with needs, ensuring not only a great time, but providing a gift that keeps on giving. The festival is sponsored by the Whirlpool Hispanic Network.

Light up the Bluff

Lake Bluff Park (Along Lake Boulevard)
St. Joseph, MI 49085

December 1 - February 1

The holiday lights shine during Light up the Bluff. Every winter, the city of St. Joseph decorates the entire length of Lake Bluff Park with lights. Trees are wrapped in blue lights and three-foot wide snowflakes hang from branches. Lights outline winter figures such as reindeer, skaters, and carolers. The entrance near the Krasl Art Center has a huge archway with "Light up the Bluff" in cursive script. Down at the other end, the Maids of the Mist fountain is decorated with cascading lights to mimic the water that flows in the summer.

You can drive the length of the park if it is windy or cold, but plenty of people enjoy strolling even in very chilly weather. Strollers and dogs on leashes are everywhere. Remember that the wind off the lake can drop the temperature on the bluff about ten degrees lower than the temperature in town. Kids do best if they are kept warm with hats, scarves, and gloves to combat the cold. Stop by the South Bend Chocolate Company or Kilwin's for hot chocolate after your walk for a perfect winter evening.

Luminary Festival

State Street
Downtown St. Joseph
www.sjtoday.org

One Friday in late November
Dusk - 9 pm

The St. Joseph Luminary Festival lets you get a jump on your winter holiday shopping while supporting the downtown businesses. Volunteers set out over 800 candles in paper bags along both sides of State Street. Christmas trees and twinkle lights add to the decor. On years where the weather is good, the Festival can get very crowded. Consider bringing a stroller or wagon for smaller kids, but pick one that can maneuver easily along packed sidewalks. Most merchants stay open late for the Festival, and some serve snacks or drinks. However, families can find it hard to squeeze inside the stores, and restaurants often have a long wait. It's a good idea to have a substantial snack or dinner before you arrive if the younger members of your party will get grouchy without food.

Some of the top-rated kid attractions include the candy-making in the window at Kilwin's, a tour of the Toy Company, and the window display at the G&M Variety store. Also, the horse-drawn trolley from the Upton Foundation offers free rides down State Street. The Luminary Festival is put on by St. Joseph Today with the help of corporate sponsors. Check their website for the exact date each year.

Magical Ice Carving Festival

Downtown St. Joseph
St. Joseph, MI 49085
www.sjtoday.org

Valentine's Day Weekend

St. Joseph's annual Magical Ice Carving Festival offers some terrific kid-friendly features. It is always cold on the bluff in the middle of February so bundle up warmly and stroll the downtown streets. Professional ice carvers create amazing displays. The chainsaws can be quite loud, so prepare shy little ones in advance. This past year, a heated hospitality tent on Pleasant Street offered hearty winter fare, hot and cold beverages, and live entertainment Friday and Saturday nights.

Magical Ice Carving Festival (cont.)

Activities for children typically feature magic shows at the Krasl, the Maud Preston Palenske Library, and the Curious Kids Museum. Each location also has projects and crafts. The times are staggered, so it's possible to attend each show in sequence. Plan to get there well in advance; seating is limited and usually the children sit up close on the ground for the best view. Box lunches are generally sold at the midday show, and the local shops also do a brisk business.

Nimby Pond Snowmobile Lake Run

11470 Hills Road
Buchanan, MI
269-369-4268

Once or twice a summer

You may not have realized that snowmobiles have their uses in the summer, too. If you get them going really fast, say, 60 miles an hour, they can skim across the top of a body of water. Of course, if you lose forward momentum, or hit a competitor's wake, you'll sink like a stone. That's the attraction in "lake running," which you can witness once or twice a year on Mark Schutze's farm. In 2007, an estimated 1,000 people showed up to watch 40 contestants race one-on-one across the 600-foot long man-made pond. Vendors offer grilled fare, sweet corn and pop; BYOB is permitted. Bring lawn chairs and blankets for a place to sit. There is a kids' program, and for a fee, you can take a helicopter tour over the farm and surrounding countryside. Admission in 2008 was $10; kids ten and under are free.

Directions: Take Cleveland Ave. south and make a slight left on Stevensville-Baroda Rd. Turn left on Hills Rd. In 2 1/2 miles, turn right to stay on Hills Rd. Destination will be on your right in another mile.

Reindog Parade

Downtown St. Joseph
www.sjtoday.org

First Saturday in December

▶

Reindog Parade (cont.)

On the first Saturday of December, St. Joseph Today hosts the annual Reindog Parade in downtown St. Joseph. It's a great time to bundle up (the snow is usually flying by then and it can be very cold) and dress your favorite pooch like Santa, Rudolph or whatever strikes your holiday imagination. This unique and fun parade features festively-dressed dogs, bands, carolers and fun floats. The parade begins at 11:30 a.m. on the north end of State Street and concludes by Santa's house at the corner of Pleasant and State Streets. Children can visit Santa at the end of the parade and if you're up for it, you and your family can take a tour of "Michigan's most romantic city" via horse-drawn trolley.

The parade is outside, but there are plenty of restroom options along the way, including at the St. Joe Today office, the public restrooms on the Bluff Park and some of the downtown shops. Parking typically isn't an issue and is usually available in any of the free lots, as well as on the side streets.

A few tips: 1) Encourage your children to ask the dog's owner if it is OK to approach his or her dog. This is a great time to teach your child, no matter how young, how to safely approach a strange dog. 2) Be sure to get your dog accustomed to its costume before parade day. Otherwise you may have a dog that will not wear the costume or will not walk in it. 3) It is cold for everyone involved, including your dog, so dress him or her warmly and bring along a couple of blankets for added warmth. 4) Be prepared for your dog to encounter horses, Shetland ponies, miniature horses, and very large and very small dogs. Also be prepared that people will likely walk up to your dog without warning.

In 2009, the Save-A-Stray organization and pet-friendly Silver Beach Hotel started "Bark for Breakfast," a continental breakfast for humans and canines. Pets eat free with owner purchase. Breakfast is served between 10 and 11 a.m., giving you and your family (Fido included) time to queue up for the parade by 11:30 a.m. "Bark for Breakfast" continues to serve hot chocolate and coffee at its coffee bar until 12:45 p.m. to help keep you nice and toasty.

St. Joseph Harvest Festival

Downtown St. Joseph
www.sjtoday.org

One Saturday in early October; check website for details

St. Joseph Harvest Festival (cont.)

Say goodbye to summer each year at the St. Joseph Harvest Festival. This is a great, low-key outing for kids. Local businesses put out colorful fall displays with painted pumpkins, whimsical scarecrows and other decorations. There's a working old-fashioned cider press, which can swarm with yellow jackets after a few hours. The cider is unpasteurized and not available for tasting, but kids enjoy seeing the apples mashed into pulp. One of the popular attractions is the petting zoo, where kids can pet bunnies, goats and other small farm animals. Bring a bottle of hand sanitizer along; you'll also need it after the pony rides along Lake Bluff Park (a small fee is charged for this attraction.) Finally, get tasting tickets for the Chili Cook-off, and sample the entries from area restaurants. The last farmer's market of the season coincides with the Harvest Festival each year. Since it covers a few blocks, consider bringing a wagon to haul children, as well as any goodies you happen to purchase.

Venetian Festival

Waterfront in St. Joseph, MI 49085
www.venetian.org

Yearly, in July

The Venetian Festival is a four-day community celebration of life on the waterfront that takes place on the bluff and near Silver Beach in St. Joseph each July. There are musical performances by both local and nationally-known artists along Lake Bluff park, at the River Stage on the St. Joseph river, and at the beautiful Shadowland Pavilion near the beach. The variety is spectacular, covering the spectrum from local dance and gymnastic troupes to The Bangles and Billy Squier.

In addition to musical performances, there are many other events for children and adults alike. For example, there is a sand-sculpture contest on the beach, a 10K River Walk and Run, beach volleyball tournaments, and a marathon swim. Aside from organized competitions, there are kids' games on the bluff, a classic car show, a craft show, and a big band dance. A highlight for many is the Taste of Southwest Michigan, which includes 50 vendors selling everything from fresh fruit smoothies to BBQ ribs to chocolate-dipped cheesecake, not to mention a wine-tasting that usually takes place on the first night of the festival.

No family festival would be complete without a carnival, and the Venetian

Venetian Festival (cont.)

Festival includes a great one with rides and games galore. Finally, in true Venetian flavor, there is a classic boat show and lighted boat parade, preceding a glorious fireworks display.

This 30-year old festival attracts over 200,000 spectators. To avoid the hassle of parking, families can park in one of the remote lots in St. Joseph or Benton Harbor, and take a free shuttle to enjoy the festival. Admission to the festival is free, with events, competitions, and food priced separately. In the past, a Passport Pin has been available for purchase, which gains admission to any concert event.

Winter Ice Festival

Downtown Watervliet
www.watervliet.biz

One weekend in January

This is a nice festival with a small-town feel. Downtown Watervliet is decorated with ice sculptures in front of most of the area businesses. Stop by the fire station for the chili cookoff, or enter the 5K fun run. The 2010 festival featured fireworks, which were a huge hit with the little kids. Since it gets dark so much earlier in winter, these are not too far past bedtime. Bundle the kids up in winter gear over their jammies and drive downtown. Park in the Harding's market lot and enjoy a terrific view; the fireworks start promptly at 8 pm. Then let the kids fall asleep as you drive home and carry them to bed. The next morning, the serious ice sculptors put on a demonstration. We did not spot any vendors or porta-potties, but area businesses are open during the festival.

Directions: From I-94, take exit 41, Main St/MI-140N. Downtown Watervliet is a half mile down Main St.

NOTES:

INTRODUCTION

Montessori classroom materials are designed to be pleasing to the eye and touch. They are crafted from wood, polished metal, and natural fibers. The classroom environment is carefully planned to welcome the children and engage all their senses as they explore and learn. As children come to appreciate the sensory appeal of the materials that surround them, they want to create their own beautiful objects. The craft stores described in this chapter are a wonderful source for fabrics, beads, and fibers that will serve as the raw materials for your family's artistic endeavors.

Gotta Go Pottery

516 Broad St.
St. Joseph, MI 49085
269-983-3300

Monday - Saturday 11 am - 6 pm
Sunday noon - 6 pm

Gotta Go Pottery is a popular place for kids looking to create a special keepsake. The store offers an enormous range of unpainted pottery objects, all of which can be painted with bright colors and personalized. Choose from plates, bowls, decorative boxes, cars, trucks, animals, piggy banks and more. There are two types of paints available, acrylic and glaze. The acrylics produce a matte finish when fired and the colors are a bit more intense. Glazed items wind up with a shiny appearance, and there is a broader range of colors from which to choose. There is a charge to purchase the unpainted item, with smaller figurines available for less than $10. There is also an hourly studio charge, which covers the cost of the painting and firing. You'll need to make a second trip later in the week to pick up your item after it has been fired; if you're visiting from out of town, Gotta Go can ship it to your home when it's ready.

The studio space offers high tables and stools. Younger children can use the smaller tables in the other section of the store, where the Hug and Stuff animals are displayed. The store also has a mosaic studio, where you can cover pre-cut letters or decorative shapes with bright bits of tile. Mosaic studio time is $10/hr. Gotta Go has thoughtfully provided a small play space for younger

Gotta Go Pottery (cont.)

children who lose interest in their projects; there are some puzzles and books there for them to browse.

Gotta Go offers birthday party packages. Some pottery items can also be customized with letter cut-outs; this requires some advance notice.

Just Bead It

312-A State St.
St. Joseph, MI 49085
269-982-4043
www.just-bead-it.com

Monday - Saturday 11 am - 6 pm
Sunday noon - 5 pm
Extended hours in the summer; call or check the website.

Check out the fabulous bead selection at this bright cheerful store in downtown St. Joseph. They have beads in an amazing array of materials and styles. If you're just starting out with bead crafts, there are plastic beads in every color, shape and size imaginable. For more sophisticated creations, they have beads in glass, semiprecious stones, shells, wood, metals and ceramics, to name a few. There's also a large selection of beads that are pre-portioned and temporarily strung, so you know you'll have enough for a specific necklace or bracelet length. Of course, they have a full range of jewelry-making supplies as well. If you're inspired by all the beautiful beads but have no idea how to start, the store has projects on display to give you ideas. There are magazines to browse, and you can also sign up for a private class.

Just Bead It allows you to book beading parties. Reservations are required and a reasonable fee covers use of the space, design guidance, and placement of the clasp on your finished projects. Parties are not suitable for children under seven, but older children should enjoy it a great deal. The cost of the beads is not covered in the party fee. You bring your own food and party favors.

Ivelise's Yarn Shop

154 East Napier St.
Benton Harbor, MI 49022
269-925-0451
www.ivelisesyarnshop.com

Monday - Friday 10:30 am - 5:30 pm
Saturday 10:30 am - 5 pm
Closed Sundays

Serious knitters will want to check out Ivelise's Yarn Shop, directly across from Fairplain Junior High in Benton Harbor. The yarn shop has been a neighborhood institution for the last forty-five years. Ivelise (pronounced Eve-a-LEASE), originally from Cuba, has created a community for knitters aged seven to eighty. On entering the clean, bright shop, you'll find yarns stacked in cubbies six feet high all around the perimeter of the store. The white walls make the huge variety of colors pop. Ivelise's carries lots of natural fiber yarns, including some made with wool produced in Michigan. They have needles, patterns, and project books for inspiration.

There's a large circular work table in the center of the store. The staff help knitters plan, start, and troubleshoot their knitting projects. Coffee, tea and hot cocoa are available, and regulars often bring cookies, candies, and chips to share. At busy times, there can be hundreds of years of accumulated knitting experience gathered together, which knitters can call on in collaborative efforts. Ivelise is a huge college football fan, and several years ago she installed a big screen television in the store. It has become a tradition for knitters to gather on Saturdays to watch the games and knit. Things can get a little heated during the Michigan - Notre Dame game!

The website lists hours and current specials. Make sure to sign up for the store newletter to get more information on classes and monthly giveaways.

Directions: From I-94, take exit 28, Scottdale Rd, heading north. Make a left on East Napier Ave (there is a left turn light.) Ivelise's is on your right. There is a parking lot adjacent to the store.

Lemon Creek Fabrics

119 W. Ferry Street
Berrien Springs, MI 49103
269-473-2201

Sunday - Wednesday noon - 6 pm
Thursday - noon - 9 pm

If you are just starting in fabric crafts, try the big chains such as Joanne's or Michael's. However, for the serious fabric crafter, there is a store in Berrien Springs that most quilters would give their best sewing machine to be able to visit regularly. Lemon Creek Fabrics has been selling ultra high-end fabrics at deep discounts since 1993. How good a discount? Mohair velvet that retails for $200/yard can be had for $30. Forty percent of their sales are snapped up by interior decorators and textile designers, and they've received rave reviews for their quality and pricing from Lake and Michigan Blue Magazines. Even without an Internet presence, they ship to artists around the country. If you have a project that needs that luxe touch on a discount budget, they sell remaindered fabrics at $0.75 per square foot. Step into their jewel-box storefront and get inspired.

Directions: From US-31, take exit 15, M-139 into the Village of Berrien Springs. Lemon Creek Fabrics is at the intersection with Ferry St, on your left. Park on either street.

Red Purl

207 North 2nd Street
Niles, MI 49120
269-684-0411
www.redpurlknits.com

Mondays and Thursdays noon - 7 pm
Fridays noon - 9 pm
Saturdays 10 am - 2 pm
Sundays 1 pm - 5 pm
Closed Tuesdays, Wednesdays, and the last Sunday of the month

Red Purl occupies a cozy storefront in downtown Niles, just off Main Street. Two friendly life-sized sheep stand in the window to greet you. Inside, you'll find a terrific selection of natural fiber yarns, with a focus on wool and

Red Purl (cont.)

organic cottons. Some of the skeins are hand-spun, and they even carry their own house brand of Alpaca yarn. They have a nice selection of books and magazines to browse for ideas; all are always 10% off list price. The store also carries a full range of knitting needles and felting supplies. They try not to overlap yarn inventory with Ivelise's Yarn Shop in Benton Harbor, so if you can't find what you're looking for in one shop, try the other.

Check their website for the class schedule. The second Sunday of each month is "Block of the Month." Designed for those with some knitting experience, the class meets once a month to work on a square of a desginated pattern. Over the course of twelve months, you'll accumulate enough blocks in complementary styles to create your own afghan. Block of the Month is a free class, but you must purchase your materials at the store. This class attracts lots of experienced knitters, who are always willing to brainstorm on ideas for your project. Red Purl also offers beginner classes and special topics such as cabled mittens and socks. There's a 10% discount for class materials. Call ahead to reserve your space in a class.

Directions: From US-31, take exit 5, Niles-Buchanan Rd, towards Niles. Niles-Buchanan Rd becomes Grant St. Make a left onto N Lincoln Ave, then a right

Trade Winds Beads

336 N. Main Street
Watervliet, MI 49098
269-463-8281

Monday - Saturday 10 am - 5 pm

Trade Winds Beads has truly everything you'll ever need for a beading project. They have a wonderful selection of loose beads from which to choose, in every material and style imaginable. Pick up a plastic box, a notepad and pen. As you make your choices, note down the price and amount of each type. At the end, they'll total your bill. The store has walls and walls of bead strands in every size, color, and shape. They also have a terrific selection of seed beads in tubes. Trade Winds has a comprehensive stock of books and project outlines. If jewelry making isn't for you, learn about working on a bead loom (you can buy small looms here) or applique. They carry a variety of beading

Trade Winds Beads (cont.)

magazines and have back issues for sale. Finally, for those that want to make their own glass beads, the store has everything you need for lampwork, including glass rods in over forty colors and the required tools. There is a small workspace in the back which customers can use as they complete their projects. In the past, the owners have offered a class in beginning beadwork; it doesn't hurt to ask if you have a truly interested group.

Directions: From I-94, take exit 41 onto MI 140N/ S Main St. Travel 0.8 miles into downtown Watervliet. Trade Winds Beads will be on your right.

INTRODUCTION

Entrepreneurship is a significant curricular consideration for Montessori students. At Brookview, children practice the life skill of counting money from a young age, and beginning in the Upper Elementary classroom, they raise money through various business practices. Past fund-raisers have included cooking and selling fresh applesauce and apple pie, a jewelry business, and constructing and selling eye-pillows for use in yoga. In Middle School, the students study economics, both on a governmental level and on the personal level of balancing a checkbook. It is also a good thing for children to get out in the community and observe the way businesses operate. The shopping districts of Berrien County are quite diverse in their offerings. Great stores abound without venturing too far.

Antiques on the Bluff

Lake Bluff Park
St. Joseph, MI 49085
www.sjcity.com

First Sunday of the month, May - October
10 am - 3 pm

During the warmer months, antique dealers from across the state descend on Lake Bluff Park on the first Sunday of the month. Antiques on the Bluff has something for every taste and budget, and offers browsing at its finest. Take advantage of the free parking lots in downtown St. Joseph. You'll need to find a good place to cross the street, since the booths line both sides of the sidewalk travelling the length of the park. Glassware and china are always popular items, and there are usually a few dealers in fine wooden furniture. This is also the place to search through old postcards and magazines. Several more eclectic dealers sell polished stones, pressed tin lithograph signs, and country crafts. Carry cash to make transactions go more smoothly, and consider pulling a wagon to carry your treasures back to the car. The hotdog cart and the city bathrooms at the center of park stay busy during this monthly event.

Everybody's Everything

1523 Niles Avenue
St. Joseph, MI 49085
269-983-3276
www.everybodyseverythingcostumes.com

Hours: Call first!
Their hours are limited and seem to be slightly sporadic.

Whether you're dressing up for Halloween, need a costume for the school play, are looking for a unique (gag) gift, or you need some new jeans; this is the place for you. Everybody's Everything was started as a consignment shop but the owner couldn't give up her fashion designer roots and began making costumes. Now you can find great vintage clothes, any costume you or your child can dream up, wigs, make-up, crazy glasses, shoes and so much more. Items are for sale or for rent.

Just across Niles Avenue from Milton Park in St. Joseph, you'll find this shop worth stopping in just for fun. The windows are painted with garish colors, and the outfitted display mannequins change outfits every couple days to coincide with local events or holidays. The door frame is covered with an interesting mosaic of items and is worth a look even if the shop is closed.

Directions: From I-94, take exit 27, Niles Ave, heading north. Travel 3.3 miles; Everybody's Everything will be on your right. There is parking behind the building.

I Love Toy Trains Store

16 S. Smith St.
New Buffalo, MI
1-800-892-2822
www.tmbv.com

Memorial Day - Labor Day: Open daily 11 am - 5 pm
September - January 1: Thursday - Sunday 11 am - 5 pm
January - May: Friday - Sunday 11 am - 5 pm

The I Love Toy Trains Store is located in a charming wood-shingled house. Climb the steps and enter the enclosed front porch, and you'll start to see the amazing selection that awaits train buffs inside. The store focuses on Lionel

I Love Toy Trains Store (cont.)

and Thomas & Friends lines, and they seem to have just about everything.

You can pick out a specialty car or two, or an entire ready-to-run boxed set. We were especially tempted by the Hogwarts Express. While this can become an expensive hobby, the store is very approachable if you are just starting out.

This is also the home of the "I Love Toy Trains" videos, which have sold over 2 million copies and won a Parent's Choice award. The store carries their entire line, including the John Deere series, and a few instructional videos on how to build a model railway layout. If you and your kids feel the need to dress the part, pick up an engineer's hat or a sweatshirt.

Kids will especially love the chance to see the toy trains in action. An oval track is suspended from the ceiling; two trains run on request. Don't miss the room in the back of the store, where a multi-tiered layout includes a tunnel, mountain, and seasonal elements. A row of buttons along the base allows kids to turn on lights and other features.

If your kids like trucks instead of trains, there are videos and toys to suit. There is a whole section devoted to John Deere toys. You can also get die-cast cars in a huge variety - we saw many different 50's and 60s classic styles, Humvees, and ice-cream trucks complete with cones. Grownups who are still young at heart will enjoy the nostalgic pressed tin toys. Finally, the store offers train repair and custom built sets; inquire for details when you visit.

Directions: From I-94, take exit 1 heading north into New Buffalo. Make a right on La Porte Rd. Continue onto S. Whittaker. Turn lef at W. Buffalo. Take 3rd left onto S. Smith St; the store is part of a shopping cluster called Lookout Landing, and off-street parking is available.

J&W Model Trains

6450 E. Becht Road
Coloma, MI 49038
269-468-5586
www.jwmodeltrains.com

Call for hours
Trains run 2nd and 4th Saturday of each month, May - September

J&W Model Trains (cont.)

For the serious train hobbyist, J&W Model Trains is a must-see. They offer a number of scale sizes, including "G," "HO," "O" and "N" trains. The store is a little intimidating if you're new to the world of model trains, but the owner has been doing this for forty years, so if you have a question, just ask. The store also serves as the headquarters for the Southwestern Michigan Garden Railroad club. Families who like to watch model trains run should make sure to visit on the days of club meetings. Behind the store is a large outdoor layout with multiple tracks, trestles and tunnels. The club members (ages range from 12 to 82) work to perfect features such as a waterfall, model town and running stream. Ask for the date of the "open house" when calling ahead - this is when club members brings their own trains, ensuring there will be plenty of action to see on the track. The public is welcome to come watch the trains run.

Directions: From I-94, take exit 39 heading north into Coloma. Veer right onto Paw Paw Lake Road, then take the left fork onto North Coloma Road. Make a left onto East Becht Road. J&W Model trains is on your immediate left, across from Washington Elementary School. It is located in an outbuilding next to a private residence, so look closely for the sign on the mailbox.

La Dee Da Children's Boutique

314 State Street
St. Joseph, MI 49085
269-983-7230
www.shopladeeda.com

Winter hours
Monday - Wednesday 11 am - 5 pm
Thursday - Friday 11 am - 6 pm
Saturday 10 am - 6 pm
Sunday noon - 5 pm

Summer hours
(June - early September):
Monday - Wednesday 10am - 7 pm
Thursday - Saturday 10 am - 8 pm
Sunday 11 am - 6 pm

Located in downtown St. Joseph, this adorable store is owned and operated by a husband-and-wife team. It features an large selection of high-quality baby and children's products, including skin care products by Mustela, Bum Genius diapers, clothing and shoes from a variety of designers, unique toys and plenty of decorative items for that special child's room. Chances are, if Suri or Shiloh's been photographed wearing it, playing with it, or sitting on it, La Dee Da carries it. If you prefer your own style choices, you can have your own frames or signs with a special phrase custom designed and produced with a two-day turnaround.

La Dee Da Children's Boutique (cont.)

The store is jam-packed with goodies, so while there's room to maneuver a small stroller, you may want to consider a carrier or holding your small children. The owner has provided a small play space for kids to allow you more browsing time. La Dee Da also offers website shopping with very fast shipping.

Perennial Accents

220 State Street
St. Joseph, MI 49085
269-983-5791
www.perennialaccents.com

Monday - Saturday 10 am - 6 pm
Sunday 11 am - 5 pm

Perennial Accents is a unique store in downtown St. Joseph that offers a variety of items. In their home section, they offer home accents, furniture, artwork, exquisite floral arrangements, and table top decor. In the garden area, there are birdhouses, birdfeeders, flags, garden accents, gazing globes, tools, windchimes and more. In their kitchen section you can find bakeware, cookbooks, cookware, countertop appliances by KitchenAid, gourmet foods, linens and gadgets. They also offer culinary classes in gourmet cooking - check their website for a current schedule. They occasionally offer classes for kids and other beginning cooks, which fill up quickly. During the holiday season they offer a wide variety of artificial lighted Christmas trees and all the decorations you will ever need to decorate your home for the holidays.

Sawyer Home & Garden Center

5865 Sawyer Road
Sawyer, MI 49125
269-426-8810
www.sawyergardencenter.com

Open 7 days per week 8 am - 8 pm (Winter 9 am - 7 pm)

Sawyer Home & Garden Center seems to have a little bit of everything! As the name suggests, the core business centers around products for the home and garden. However, that is a pretty broad category, considering just about

Sawyer Home & Garden Center (cont.)

everything can be used in the home and garden. It would be easier to list the things you cannot find at this store. The store carries a great selection and many top brands of the latest tools, outdoor furniture, grills, nursery stock and all the related products.

In addition to the typical home and garden products, the store's unique character shines in the form of its vast gift shop (including toys for the kids), huge selection of wines and craft-brewed beer, seasonal produce with an emphasis on local products, gourmet cheeses, organic dairy products, specialty salsas, sauces and dips, steaks and chops, fresh baked bread, pasta, specialty dessert items including the best homemade pies around and much, much more. Stop by on the weekends for cooking demonstrations by Chef Joe using in-house products, with many of the prepared items available to sample and for purchase.

Product offerings change with the holidays and the seasons. Whether you are looking for a new shrub for your front yard, plants for your family garden, a nice bottle of wine, a gift for Mom or a goumet food item, Sawyer Home & Garden Center is your destination.

Directions: From I-94, take exit 12 and go 1/2 mile east.

Shipshewana

Shipshewana, IN
www.shipshewana.com

Shops open every day except Sunday

If you are interested in the Amish and their culture, this is the place to visit! Shipshewana is the third largest Amish community in the United States. Authentic Amish quilts and handmade Amish furniture are just some of the goods available in the many shops. There are Amish grocery stores where the Amish have ground the spices themselves and made broths into powders to be sold. Several restaurants serve traditional Amish food. Horses and buggies are used extensively, so be careful where you step!

It's really like stepping back in time to visit Shipshewana. For example, some stores still have gas lamps because they hold true to their beliefs of no electricity. Don't miss the theater where the story of the Amish Mennonites is told.

Shipshewana (cont.)

Plan to stay at one of the many B&B's because you can't see all Shipshewana has to offer in one day. It's a beautiful town packed full of interesting history.

Directions: Take US-31 south toward South Bend. Continue east on US-20. Turn left on IN-5 to Shipshewana. The drive is about 1 1/2 hours from St. Joseph.

The Toy Company

208 State Street
Saint Joseph, Michigan 49085
269-983-0600

Summer: Monday - Saturday 10 am - 9 pm,
Sunday noon - 9 pm

Winter: Monday - Wednesday 10 am - 6 pm,
Thursday and Friday 10 am - 8 pm,
Saturday 10 am - 6 pm, Sunday noon - 5 pm

We've all had to scramble at the last minute for a present for a birthday party. Next time this happens to you, head straight to The Toy Company. They do a brisk business on Saturday mornings as procrastinating partygoers pick from their great selection, then take advantage of the free gift wrapping service. The Toy Company focuses on educational toys for ages infant to 80 and beyond. Some of their big lines include Playmobile, Melissa and Doug, Webkinz, and Thomas the Tank Engine. There's also a wide range of puzzles and board games, a small alcove of quality books (including the I Can Read classics) and a long wall of little gadgets that make terrific stocking stuffers or party favors.

Kids love coming to The Toy Company, and the store puts a lot of thought into making it a welcoming place. There are tables arranged for play throughout the store, including an impressive train set. The bathroom is a godsend for a harried family. We love the recommendations from the store staff. Give them the age of the child and your price range, and they have never failed to come up with a fantastic idea. Combine these features with a selection of toys that you can't buy in any of the big-box chain stores, and it's easy to see why The Toy Company is a family favorite.

NOTES:

INTRODUCTION

The Montessori curriculum follows a three year cycle, a common underlying theme across diverse disciplines. As the school's study of history, geography, music and art travels through the cycle, each of the continents is covered in turn. We are fortunate to have a diverse student body, which enriches our children's study of different cultures. Local foods are always a popular element of the lesson plan. The specialty food markets described in this chapter give everyone a chance to try some regional delicacies. And since our school seems to contain a great many chocolate lovers, we have an extra section on all the places to get wonderful local candies.

Apple Valley Market and Natural Foods

9067 US 31
Berrien Springs, MI 49103
269-471-3234
www.avnf.com

Monday - Thursday 7 am - 11 pm
Friday 7 am - 4 pm (winter), 7 am - 6 pm (summer)
Closed Saturdays

Now a chain with six locations, Apple Valley got its start in Berrien Springs in 1919, when it was the College Supply Store for Emmanuel Missionary College. The college went on to become Andrews University, while the store became Apple Valley Market and Natural Foods. Andrews University sold the store in 1998, but it retains its Seventh-Day Adventist character.

When you first enter the market, you'll find de Cafe 31 to your immediate right. This small eatery offers hot coffee drinks, gourmet vegetarian sandwiches such as hummus and roasted portobello, as well as breakfast entrees. Free WiFi is available inside the cafe, and pitchers of iced tea and lemonade on the counter add a homey touch. Passing through into the market itself, the store is divided into two areas -- a traditional-style supermarket on the left and the area's broadest selection of natural foods on the right. In the supermarket section, you'll find outstanding produce, including organic vegetables from the Andrews University gardens.

In the natural foods section, you'll find a wide range of specialty juices and

Apple Valley Market and Natural Foods (cont.)

teas. Three entire aisles are devoted to bulk grains, flours, beans and dried fruits. Most of these are Apple Valley's own brand, minimally packaged in plastic sacks, but Bob's Red Mill and Hodgson Mills products also are available. There are lots of organic and natural cookies, crackers, chips, and cereals. In keeping with Seventh-Day Adventist beliefs, there is no meat for sale in the store. However, an entire aisle of meat substitutes is available, and Apple Valley's advertising flyers usually carry simple recipes that use these products or can help make vegetarian versions of your favorite meat recipes. You also can find environmentally-friendly cleaning products, Earth's Best diapers and organic baby food. Apple Valley has an enormous selection of vitamins and herbal supplements. The back corner carries a selection of books, mostly devoted to alternative health. There also is a small selection of juicers, food mills and dehydrators.

Finally, you also can drop off and pick up your dry cleaning at Apple Valley; services are provided by Sanitary Cleaners in St. Joseph.

Directions: From US-31, take exit 15A, Old 31 South, into Berrien Springs. Apple Valley is on the left, across from the Berrien County Fairgrounds.

Niles Bensidoun French Market

Corner of Front and Main Streets
Niles, MI 49120
www.nilesmainstreet.org

Late May - Early October
Thursdays and Saturdays 9 am - 2 pm

More than a farmer's market, the Niles Bensidoun French Market was developed by a French family with over fifty years experience in the open-air markets that are a hallmark of French life. Markets there serve as community gathering places, allowing residents to purchase artisanal food and crafts made in their own area. This helps the local economy and strengthens community ties. What's not to love? Niles has the only Bensidoun French market in Michigan and one of only a handful in the country, with the characteristic canopies over all the vendor booths. It's definitely worth a trip.

The roster of vendors changes a little from year to year. You can generally count on being able to purchase local vegetables, fruits, meats and flowers.

Niles Bensidoun French Market (cont.)

Lavender grows well in the Niles area and the Market is a great place to purchase products made from these fragrant flowers, including sachets and soaps. Woodworkers, jewelers, seamstresses and other artisans offer high-quality and unique items which make great gifts. The nuns from the Fraternite of Notre Dame in Chicago sell incredible pastries, but they are only there once a month, usually the first Thursday. Check the website for each year's participants.

Directions: From US-31, take Exit 5, Niles-Buchanan Rd, towards Niles. Travel 2.5 miles; the street becomes Grant St as you enter Niles. Make a left on Lincoln Ave and then take the first right onto W. Main St. You'll cross the bridge over the St. Joseph River and immediately arrive at the intersection of Front and Main.

Berrien Springs Oriental Supermarket

116 E. Ferry Street
Berrien Springs, MI 49103
269-471-5744

Monday - Thursday 9:30 am - 7 pm
Friday 9:30 am - dusk
Saturday closed
Sunday 11 am - 6 pm

On East Ferry Street in Berrien Springs, just before the bridge over the river, the Berrien Springs Oriental Supermarket occupies a small storefront. Inside, the store is packed full of food and products you just can't find in the big supermarkets. The right side of the store has a long shelf of canned and bottled Asian condiments. This is the place to get soy sauce in many varieties, chutneys, marinades and cooking sauces, and canned vegetables such as bamboo shoots and lychee fruit. The larger sizes are especially nice if you use these a lot in your cooking. The refrigerated cases contain a treat - good, fresh kimchee (Korean pickles) brought in from Chicago. This is the real deal and there are usually several varieties, including cabbage and radish. You can also get large quantities of peeled garlic cloves, local eggs, and exotic fresh vegetables like baby bok choy. The chest freezers hold potstickers, stuffed buns, and other appetizers. In the back, pick up a twenty pound bag of rice - there are many varieties such as short grain and basmati.

The market also has tableware, such as chopsticks, tea sets, sushi dishes, and

Berrien Springs Oriental Supermarket (cont.)

electric rice cookers. You can find Japanese gummy candies in flavors such as muscat grape, peach, kiwi and pineapple. Pocky sticks, a great treat from Japan, are thin breadsticks with flavored coatings such as chocolate, mocha, and strawberry. Stock turnover of some items can be slow, so check the expiration dates. The friendly staff will help you pack your items in a box and carry it out to the car for you.

Directions: From US-31, take exit 15A, Old US 31S, into Berrien Springs. Turn left on Ferry St. The supermarket is on your right.

Drier's Meat Market

14 South Elm Street
Three Oaks, MI 49128
888-521-3999
www.driers.com

Monday - Saturday 9am - 5pm
Sunday 11am - 5pm
Closed January 1 through two weeks before Easter

Not much has changed at Drier's Meat Market since it opened in 1913. Actually, there has been a butcher shop in that location since 1875, but it was in 1913 that it was purchased by the Drier family. The decor and products are very much the way they were almost a century ago. Hopefully, it will remain unchanged for the next 100 years, as you don't mess with perfection.

The third generation continues the tradition. The market offers a variety of smoked meats and cheeses. It is most noted for its ring bologna (all-beef) and spiral smoked ham. Both of these are among the favorites of celebrities and everyday people alike. Larry Hagman, Roger Ebert, and Chicago's Mayor Daley are just a few of the noteworthy customers that have shopped at Drier's.

Directions: From I-94, take exit 12 toward Sawyer. Take a left on Sawyer Rd, then the third left on 3 Oaks Rd. Travel 5.2 miles; 3 Oaks becomes Elm St. Drier's will be on your right.

Falatic's Meat Market

12236 Red Arrow Highway
Sawyer, MI 49125
269-426-3224
www.falatics.com

Wednesday - Sunday: 10 am - 5:30 pm
Open daily July and August

Falactic's Meat Market offers one of the best selections and finest quality of meat and seafood in the area. Ron and Peg Falatic, their son Nick and the entire family (everyone helps out on busy holiday weekends) provide the type of service that is rare in this era of processed, prepackaged and hurry up lifestyles. They take tremendous pride in their work and you will notice it the first time you walk in the store and place your order. After a few visits, they will no longer ask how you want your meat ground or how thick to cut your steaks, they will just know. After a few more visits, you will feel like one of the family. No wonder they've been in business since 1976. Loyal customers have brought in pennants from their alma maters all over the country; the ceiling is covered with them.

Some of the outstanding products to try: Smoked Ham and Turkey - simply great for sandwiches and other deli uses. Kids (and adults) usually get a sample as it is sliced to order. Prosciutto - this dry cured ham from Parma, Italy is sliced paper-thin to order. We think it's the best (perhaps only) available in the area. Beef - ground to order, one pound, two pounds, more fat, less fat, however you like it. Steaks - pick your cut, thickness, bone-in, bone-out, trimmed and cut to order. Chicken Polish Sausage, Chicken Bratwurst, Chicken Italian Sausage - all made in-house. Hot Dogs - regular or polish, none better, all made in-house. Whole Turkey - fresh not frozen, may need to be preordered especially around Thanksgiving where 500-600 will go out the door. If you have never had a fresh turkey you need to call and order one. Smoked Product - hams, suasage, pork chops, salmon and lots more, it is all good and all smoked in-house. Seafood - while known for their meat, a great selection of fresh and frozen seafood is also available.

A comprehensive list of all their products is available on the website or just call the shop. If they do not have it, they can get it.

Directions: From I-94, take exit 16 towards Bridgman. Travel south on Red Arrow Highway for 2.5 miles. Falatic's will be on the right.

Kim's Asian Grocery

131 N. Main Street
Watervliet, MI 49098
269-463-8112
www.kimsasiangrocery.com

Monday - Saturday 11 am - 9 pm
Closed Sundays

Love the idea of an ethnic grocer but prefer the spacious aisles offered at your neighborhood shop? Kim's Asian Market offers the best of both worlds. On the shelves you'll find authentic Asian produce, ingredients, and spices. Yet the shop strives to maintain the spacious, clean, fresh feel of other small-town grocers. One side of the store carries cold drinks and frozen foods. Among the various beverages, we spotted Mexican Coca-Cola (made with sugar instead of corn syrup), Grass Jelly Drink from Vietnam, Guarabana juice, Rice Congee from China, and Peanut Soup from Japan. There is an impressive array of frozen vegetables from India, including okra and karela bitter melon.

If you'd like to try some of these delicacies but aren't sure how to use them, pick up one of the glossy cookbooks for sale in the front of the store - they carry titles on a whole host of Asian cuisines. Kim's carries the largest bags of rice we've seen in Berrien County - some varieties are available in fifty pound sacks! They also have a great selection of dried noodles and bottled sauces. There are outdoor booths in front of the store to enjoy your treats as you watch the pedestrian traffic on Main Street. Kim's Grocery plans to add a buffet of hot foods, and there's open space in the back of the store to accomodate that later. For now, however, the selection is limited to takeout drinks and Asian snack items.

Directions: From I-94, take exit 41 towards Watervliet. Travel 0.7 miles on Main St; Kim's Asian Grocery will be on your left.

La Perla Produce, Inc.

1231 Pipestone Road
Benton Harbor, MI 49022
269-934-8813

Open seven days a week
Summer: 8:30 am- 9 pm
Winter (beginning in November): 8:30 am- 8 pm daily

If you're looking for an authentic Mexican grocery store, there's no place better than La Perla. Not only will you find typical Mexican grocery items such as adobo sauce, masa flour or melting cheese, but La Perla also has a great butcher who sells high quality arracherra (thinly sliced flank steak for grilling), chorizo, and other meats.

Locals know that La Perla is the only place to get perfectly ripe avocados and mangoes, as well as several varieties of Mexican peppers and nopales (prickly pear cactus). Kids love the traditional Mexican candy. One favorite is Pelon Pelo Rico, Spanish for "bald man - delicious hair!" It is a little plastic figurine. When you push on the bottom, a sweet and spicy chili tamarind paste comes up through the top of the head, like hair! It's kind of like an edible push-up Chia Pet. Mexican sweet pastries are available, as are packages of refrigerated tamales, with your choice of beef or chicken, perfect to take home for dinner.

La Perla is also a great place to get a delicious, inexpensive, authentic Mexican meal. The menu changes daily. Their green tomatillo salsa is to die for, and if you ask, they'll give you homemade flour tortillas with your meal. There are a small number of booths and tables in the back of the store. If you go at lunch time or right after work, it is likely to be packed with locals grabbing some tacos de carne asada or a torta especial (La Perla's specialty sandwich with several types of meats, vegetables and a delicious homemade sauce). Be sure to pick up some fresh tortilllas and chips - they're brought in from El Milagro tortilla factory in Chicago.

Directions: From I-94, take exit 29, Pipestone Rd, heading north. Travel 1.6 miles; La Perla Produce will be on your right.

Mabuhay Oriental Food Store

111 N. Cass Street
Berrien Springs, MI 49103
269-473-2755

Monday: 12 pm - 7 pm
Tuesday - Friday and Sunday: 11 am - 7 pm
Closed Saturday

Mabuhay specializes in Southeast Asian ingredients. This small, clean, well-lit store is in downtown Berrien Springs. A refrigerator case holds delicacies such as Filipino chicken sausage and preserved duck eggs. There is a small case of produce, including fresh lemongrass and Japanese eggplants. Their shelves hold a wide range of sauces and condiments from Indonesia, Thailand, Malaysia, Jamaica, Korea, and Japan. They have a particularly good selection of dried beans, flours, and noodles. This is the place to get tapioca pearls in different sizes and flavors, perfect for making the popular "bubble" teas.

Directions: From I-94, take exit 27, M-139. Follow M-139 into the Village of Berrien Springs, where it is called Cass Street. Mabuhay Oriental Food Store is on your right as you approach the intersection with Ferry Street.

Melendez Imports

124 East Ferry Street
Berrien Springs, MI 49103
269-473-3477

Monday - Wednesday 11 am - 9 pm
Thursday 10 am - 9 pm
Friday 9 am - 9 pm
Closed Saturday
Sunday 11 am - 8 pm

Andrews University in Berrien Springs draws students from all over the world. Melendez Imports keeps many of these students from getting homesick by making sure they have access to their favorite foods from home. This small ethnic grocery store concentrates on items from Africa, the Carribbean, and Central and South America. When you walk in, you will be greeted with fresh produce including plantains, coconuts, avocados, cilantro, yucca root, aloe leaves, and sugarcane stalks. The front of the store has open sacks of dried beans, peas, and chilis that can be purchased in the quantities you need.

Melendez Imports (cont.)

Melendez has an excellent selection of sodas and juices. We tried Guarana soda from Brazil - delicious! The shelves are lined with the full Goya product line, including sauces, canned fruits and vegetables, and flours. Chest freezers along the side wall hold whole frozen fish, cubed goat meat, oxtails, jute leaves, grated coconut and sugar cane. African food products include red palm oil, fufu flour, and egusi (dried watermelon seeds).

The back of the store includes a small carryout window. While Andrews is in session, this is the place to get home-cooked Jamaican food on Fridays. The menu is short, but includes classic dishes such as curry goat, oxtail stew, and red snapper. All entrees come with rice and peas and a side vegetable. For dessert, browse the candy aisle. The staff are friendly and enthusiastic about the products they carry - they can recommend a new treat or help you find something specific.

If you are interested in making some of these dishes at home, you can buy a molcajete (a Mexican mortar and pestle) and corn husks in which to wrap your tamales. Melendez accepts credit cards.

Directions: From US-1, take exit 15, M-139, into the Village of Berrien Springs, where it is called Cass Street. Make a left at the light onto Ferry Street. Melendez Imports is one block down on the right, before the bridge. Park on the street in front of the store.

St. Joseph Farmer's Market

Lake Bluff Park
St. Joseph, MI 49085

Early June - September
Saturdays 9 am - 2 pm

July and August
also Wednesdays 9 am - 2 pm

The downtown farmer's market in St. Joseph has grown remarkably in recent years. Moving the market stalls to Lake Bluff Park was a welcome change last year, preserving the parking lot to allow for easy access to the shopping. In 2010, those in search of the absolutely freshest fruits, flowers and vegetables will be able to shop twice a week, on Saturdays and Wednesdays.

St. Joseph Farmer's Market (cont.)

In addition to fresh local produce, several vendors offer fresh baked breads, pastries and pies. Handmade soaps and dried flower arrangements have also been popular. The market is an excellent source for heirloom, organic and non-hybrid varieties of vegetable plants and herbs. The selection here is vastly superior to the national hardware chains, and the nursery owners are knowledgeable and can help you find the exact plants to suit your needs. They also have ornamental plants that are selected to thrive in this region. We recommend bringing a wagon, since it's easy to buy more than you can carry.

So far, there have not been consistent offerings of eggs, cheeses, poultry and meats. Hopefully, the extended days will attract more vendors and an even broader selection of fresh and local goods.

Skip's Open-Air European Farmer's Market

16710 Lakeshore Rd
New Buffalo, MI 49117
269-469-3341
www.skipsrestaurantandcatering.info

May - Early October
Saturdays and Sundays, 9 am - 2 pm

Skip's European Open-Air Farmer's Market is a delightful weekend experience for the family. Owner Rhonda Sobecki tries to have a special attraction/booth targeted specifically to children each weekend. We have enjoyed experiences with Curious Kids, the local fire department, and farmers who bring their own petting zoos. Browse the booths, pick up some fresh fruit, wash it off with a bottle of water, and eat one of the cafe tables. There's also artisan snacks and coffee to enjoy. Skip's sets up a station to sell steak burgers, and Bit of Swiss breads with local cheeses and preserves completes the meal. A grassy area next to the market stalls gives the kids a place to run around and burn off some energy.

At the market, you'll find crafts including knit pieces, jewelry and photography. Nurseries offer flats of bedding plants and herbs for your own garden at home. Make sure to look for the lady selling homemade rum cake, a local favorite. The vendors are always willing and happy to talk about their goods, and we find that they are very patient making change with the children.

Skip's Open-Air European Farmer's Market (cont.)

Directions: From I-94, take exit 6, Union Pier Rd. Turn left at flashing light onto Red Arrow Hwy, then make a sharp right onto Lakeshore Rd. The market will be on your left. There is ample parking.

The Chocolate Garden

2691 Friday Road
Coloma, MI 49038
269-468-9866
www.chocolategarden.com

Daily 10 am - 6 pm
Closed: New Year's Day, Easter Sunday, Thanksgiving, Christmas

Forget the naked lady on the horse! This is truly remarkable chocolate. A quick five minute detour off exit 39 will take you to a charming farmhouse with the best truffles this side of Belgium. Each truffle is handmade in small batches. What makes them unique is that there is no outer shell. The smooth, creamy truffle center is rolled in chopped chocolate, and the entire treat melts in your mouth almost instantly. Featured on the Food Network and praised in many other publications, these truffles will ruin for life the occasional chocoholic, and chocolate connoisseurs will be pleasantly surprised. You can watch their reputation-making Food Network clip as it plays endlessly on the TV screen in the shop. The truffles come pre-packaged in assortment boxes; if there's a particular flavor you need to try, they offer a small bag that holds two one ounce truffles. The shop carries mugs and T-shirts as well as the chocolates. Smaller kids will need to be encouraged not to touch, but older children who appreciate wonderful chocolate will enjoy the outing.

Directions: From I-94, take exit 39, Friday Rd., turning left (away from Coloma). The Chocolate Garden is on your left; there are lots of signs to point your way.

D.W. Hammond

1697 Colfax Avenue
Benton Harbor, MI 49022
269-757-7829
www.dwhammond.com

Monday - Friday 10 am - 6 pm
Saturday 10 am - 4 pm
Closed Sunday

The Hammond family tradition of candy making started in 1885 when D.W. Hammond started selling candies in his butcher shop in Bangor. Subsequent generations kept his recipies and made candy as gifts for special friends. In 1972, the family started selling candy at local fairs and via mail order. Now, Keith Hammond, the great-grandson of D.W., has opened the first retail location since the 1880's to sell the treats made from recipies his family has developed over the decades. Ask to see the picture of the original store; a close-up is featured on their signfront. All of their candy is made on site at the store. The fudge is made from a 75-year-old recipe.

The shop's signature item is the caramel pecan turtles. These are eye-catching candies with a molded realistic turtle shape in milk chocolate. Inside, gooey caramel rests on top of a base of incredibly fresh pecans. D.W. Hammond's also has creams and nut clusters. Their version of candy bark is called "break-ups" because they pour the chocolate in a thinner layer which is easier to break into bite-sized pieces. Sugar-free chocolates are available for those on a special diet.

Those who are starting to explore the art of candy-making will find a full line of supplies here. There are chocolate wafers in nine different colors, and you can special order molds in a huge variety of shapes and sizes. The store also carries fondant and crystallized sugar, and all ingredients are fresh. If you want a special chocolate treat (like a logo) but don't want to make it yourself, they can produce custom orders.

Directions: From I-94, take exit 28, Scottdale Road, headed north. Turn left (there is a left turn light) onto Napier Avenue. Make a right onto Colfax and then make an immediate right into the parking lot.

Kilwin's

217 State Street
St. Joseph, MI 49085
269-982-1330
www.kilwins.com

Summer:
Monday - Saturday 10 am - 10 pm
Sunday noon - 10 pm.

Fall:
Monday - Thursday 10 am - 8 pm
Friday and Saturday 10 am - 9 pm
Sunday noon - 8 pm.

Winter:
Monday - Saturday 10 am - 6 pm,
Sunday noon - 6 pm

"We stay open until the last customer is served!"

The friendly staff at Kilwin's are always ready to help you indulge. This chocolate store is part of a franchise chain that started in Northern Michigan in 1947; the St. Joseph location opened in 1998. The first thing you'll see upon entering the store is the large work space in the front window. Here, the fudge is hand-paddled on marble slabs. Watching the candy-makers at work is fun for little kids, and the wall is low so they can see. The line for ice cream forms at the back of the store. Check out the ice cream truck, a remnant of a past St. Joseph summer street display. Along with the ice cream you can order some decadent hot chocolate and cider; the "drinking chocolate" is an intense four ounces and definitely a grownup's treat. If allergies are an issue, you can consult the recipe book to make sure your favorite flavor checks out. The staff will also be happy to open a fresh carton to avoid any cross-contamination.

Kilwin's is especially famous for their fudge and their caramel apples, of which they sold 12,500 last year in Saint Joseph alone! These giant, delectable apples are handmade right on the premises. Kilwin's can assemble a gift basket that includes some of their best creations. They have a lot of creative candies, such as chocolate dipped animal crackers and caramel-drizzled Rice Krispie squares, as well as traditional filled chocolates. The fudge counter is topped by a wonderful miniature carousel over two feet in diameter. Hold up your kids to let them appreciate the detail as it twirls around. Once you've made your choice, sit at the old-fashioned cafe tables inside, or head out to the outdoor benches for some people-watching.

Veni's Sweet Shop

228 East Main St
Niles, MI 49120
269-684-1323
www.venischocolate.com

Monday - Saturday 9 am - 7 pm
Sunday 12 noon - 5 pm

This past Christmas, we were delighted to have a chance to finally sample sugar plums. Veni's Sweet Shop makes these confections on their premises, along with a wide range of other wonderful treats. Veni's has been in business on the same location in downtown Niles since 1910. The Tiffany-style windows on the front of the shop welcome you to a traditional candy store. The back counter, made of burnished wood and granite, is a relic from the Chicago Worlds' Fair, and has been in the store since the 1930's. The current owners bought the store from the founding family, but took time to carefully learn all the recipes and secrets that have made Veni's popular for almost 100 years.

Some of their best-loved creations include candied orange peel drenched in dark chocolate and Oreo-flavored truffles, in addition to the aforementioned sugar plums. They have some of the best sugar-free chocolates around. Their nuts are glazed and spiced in-house, served in traditional paper cones. Of course, there's a large array of chocolate creams and meltaways. And they've had 99 years to perfect their recipe for vanilla caramels. If you're not sure what you'd like, the friendly staff is happy to give you a sample.

Not one to rest on their laurels, the chocolate makers at Veni's have been keeping up with current candy themes. No, this isn't the place to find chipotle-infused chocolate or other too-trendy flavors, but they have been making more dark chocolates with higher cacao content. They also make exquisite pieces such as chocolate birds nests, decorated with edible chocolate birds, and chocolate cups shaped like tulips. Veni's never uses waxes or other fillers in their chocolates.

Veni's will ship their chocolates across the country, and offers prepackaged gift boxes for all your gift-giving needs.

Directions: From US 31, take exit 5, Niles-Buchanan Rd, towards Niles; the street name changes to Grant Street. Cross the St. Joseph River and turn left on Third St. Veni's is at the intersection of Main and Third Streets, on your left. Street parking is available on Main Street.

INTRODUCTION

Montessori children are well-versed in the grace and courtesy of sitting at the table. Even casual lunchtime at school involves placemats, real dishes and silverware, and table manners. Taking children to restaurants allows them to show what they've learned. It's always best, however, to plan mealtime outings that allow for some beginner's mistakes. Here's a list that you can depend on so that you don't have to deprive the kids of practicing what they've learned. All of these restaurants are family-friendly and will greet your children with a smile. Bon appétit!

Bert's Breakfast Korner

2814 Kimmel St.
Stevensville, MI 49127
269-429-7349

Monday - Friday 6 am to noon
Saturday 7 am to 1 pm
Closed Sundays

This friendly, cozy, small town restaurant serves up a solid, homestyle American breakfast. Your coffee cup will barely reach 3/4 full before an extremely attentive waitress offers you a warm up. For little ones, coloring crayons are provided and the fruit is cut into perfect bite sizes. Saturdays can be busy, so arriving early will increase your chances of being seated right away.

Directions: From I-94, take exit 22. Head east on John Beers Rd towards Stevensville. Go through the stop light, crossing over Red Arrow Highway. At the next 4-way stop sign, turn right onto St. Joseph Ave. Turn right at the next street, Kimmel St. Bert's Korner is near the corner of Kimmel and Berrien Sts.

Caffe Tosi

516 Pleasant Street
St. Joseph, MI 49085
269-983-5006
www.caffetosi.com

Monday - Friday 7 am - 8 pm
Saturday 8 am - 8 pm
Sunday 8 am - 4 pm

Ann Arbor may have Zingerman's Cafe, but St. Joseph has Caffe Tosi, a taste of northern Italy. An expansion of the well-beloved Tosi's of Stevensville, the wonderful cafe atmosphere surrounds you the minute you walk through their door. The artwork on the walls are from local artists. On a cold winter day this is the spot to enjoy eating a bowl of soup, or to spend a quiet weekend morning having breakfast. The bill of fare in the mornings includes fresh pastries from the affiliated Bit Of Swiss bakery, oatmeal from steel-cut oats, pancakes, bacon, and eggs cooked to order.

Although small inside, it seats quite a few people; wrangling strollers and high chairs can be difficult due to the limited space. In the warmer months they have tables out front for you to enjoy your meal. Caffe Tosi is appropriate for small get-togethers, where you and your friends can linger over their excellent coffee, cappucinos and lattes. For lunch, choose from their extensive sandwich and panini menu, and make sure to include a side of their prepared salads. One standout is the daily minestrone, for which they are justifiably famous. Even veggie-hating kids love this soup, which can also be purchased in large containers to take home. There is always an additional daily soup, and clam chowder on Friday and Saturdays. Gourmet food items are available for purchase, including their house basalmic vinegar and specialty coffee products. Caffe Tosi accepts takeout orders by phone or fax, and offers delivery in a limited area.

Charlie's Piggin' N' Grinnin'

136 Territorial Rd
Benton Harbor, MI 49022
269-934-7675
www.piggin-n-grinnin.com

Summer Hours:
Monday: 11am - 2pm
Tuesday - Thursday: 11am - 6pm
Friday - Saturday: 11am - 8pm
Closed Sundays

Winter Hours
(end of October - March)
Monday 11am - 2pm
Tuesday - Saturday 11am - 6pm
Closed Sundays

Piggin' N' Grinnin' has a great eclectic feel to it. Best of all, pigs are everywhere! Pig figurines, little pig statues, antique toys pig, pictures of pigs, posters of pigs - it goes on and on. Want a fun activity to keep your little ones busy while you get a bite or two in for yourself? Ask them to count how many pigs they see in the restaurant. It works every time.

At each table is a whole roll of paper towel so you don't have to worry about getting too messy with the three different types of BBQ sauce provided. Sweet and Mild is perfect for kids, while most adults will enjoy the Spicy. The third style, Horseradish, is a unique taste and should not be missed. The meat is slow cooked for hours at relatively low temperatures, just as real BBQ is meant to be made. Place your order at the counter and take it to your table. There always seems to be friendly staff that will help with cleanup, another bonus when dining with children.

Charlie and Susan do most of their business during the week, especially during lunchtime. That means if you go during the weekend, you don't have to worry about your kids disturbing others. In fact, chances are you'll see Charlie or Susan doing some bookwork out at a table. Introduce yourself to them - they're wonderfully friendly. If you need to pick up a large order late in the evening, call ahead - chances are they will stay open late for you.

Directions: From I-94, take exit 29, Pipestone Rd, towards Benton Harbor. After 3 1/2 miles, Pipestone becomes Water St after crossing Main St in downtown Benton Harbor. Take the immediate right onto Territorial Rd; Piggin' N' Grinnin' is on the first block.

Clementine's Too

1235 Broad Street
St. Joseph, MI 49085
269-983-0990
www.ohmydarling.com

Monday - Thursday 11 am - 9 pm
Friday - Saturday 11 am - 10 pm
Sunday noon - 9 pm

This kid-friendly restaurant is located on the St. Joseph River. The décor is nautical with a long wooden bar and high-backed booths. Clementine's Too (the original Clementine's is in nearby South Haven) offers an American menu with something for everyone: pasta, sandwiches, salads, steaks, fried shrimp, burgers and more. They're known for their perch, which you can get as a sandwich or a dinner. The onion rings come stacked in a tower on a tall wooden stick, served with ranch dressing for dipping. Finish your meal with their signature hot apple dumpling a la mode.

The best thing about Clementine's (besides the onion rings) is that in the summer, you can sit outside and watch the boats go by. If there is a long wait, it's fun to walk down the pier and look at the boats with your kids until your table is ready. In cooler weather, the restaurant offers crayons for coloring. The kid's menu includes fresh-sliced apples and fried shrimp. There's a changing table in the bathroom. They do not accept reservations, so on summer days, it's probably best to have some portable activities to keep the kids busy as you wait for a table.

Directions: From Main St. in downtown St. Joseph, turn onto Broad St, travelling away from Lake Michigan. Clementine's Too will be on your left, on the water.

Dino's Family Restaurant and Pancake House

2939 Niles Avenue
St. Joseph, MI 49085
269-982-0229

Monday - Friday, 6 am - 4 pm
Saturday and Sunday, 7 am - 3 pm
Extended dinner hours in the summer

Dino's Family Restaurant and Pancake House(cont.)

The Tripodis family have been serving up meals for St. Joseph residents since 1973. Dino's is located on Niles Avenue, near Hilltop. They have a dedicated group of regulars that show up each week for their breakfasts. The menu covers two densely typed pages and includes omelets, pancakes, eggs with side meats, crepes, and blintzes. The kid's menu offers a number of right-sized portions, such as a half serving of French toast or a pancake with a sausage link. The coffee is hot and the friendly waitresses keep your mug filled. There are plenty of highchairs and booster seats available. It can get busy on Sunday mornings, but there's plenty of parking and rarely a wait for a table. Sandwiches for lunch include deli fare such as Reubens, giant salads, and grilled items like burgers and hot open sandwiches. A case near the door lets you check out the daily selection of pies, which always includes a tray of Greek baklava.

Directions: From downtown St. Joseph, take Main St. headed south. Veer left onto Niles Ave. Dino's will be on your left, just past the Dairy Queen.

Golden Brown Bakery and Cafe

201 State Street
St. Joseph, MI 49085
269-983-2002
www.goldenbrownbakery.com

Monday - Friday 6:30 am - 5 pm
Saturday 6:30 am - 6 pm
Sunday (summer only) 6:30 am - 2 pm

The Golden Brown Bakery and Cafe anchors the north end of State Street. All of their pastries and cookies are brought in fresh daily from the main bakery in South Haven. In addition to cookies, danishes and scones, they offer panini sandwiches and salads, making it a nice place to stop for a quick bite to eat. They also offer an assortment of excellent homemade soups and the selection changes daily. There are eight tables and the cafe seats about twenty people total. The bathroom does not have a changing table, but is large enough to easily accommodate a stroller.

The Livery

190 5th Street
Benton Harbor, MI 49022
269-925-8760
www.liverybrew.com

Monday - Thursday: 4 pm - midnight
Friday: 11:30 am - midnight
Saturday: noon - 1 am
Sunday: 2 pm - 9pm

This is one of the easiest places to bring the family if you just want to chat with friends over a beer. You won't find diaper changing stations in the restrooms or booster seats but nonetheless, this is a family-friendly brewery.

The bar and cafe are located at the lower level, whcih features a giant array of games for all ages. The menu in the restaurant changes, but you'll always find a hot pretzel or pretzel nuggets on the menu. Other options may include soup, pizzas, hummus, nachos, burritos and more. If you're lucky, you may even stumble onto ethnic food night at the Livery. Beverages for children are limited to very sugary soda pops or the self-serve cooler of water that sits just inside the door. Outside, the beer garden isn't terribly spacious, but it has numerous picnic tables and yard chairs. In the warmer months you may enjoy a game of corn hole. This is a great place to let the kids get their wiggles out.

The Livery's second floor features a stage where you can catch great live acts. Be aware that most of the music is too loud for young ears. The third floor balcony offers a small gallery with changing exhibitions. When you hear the trains roll through downtown Benton Harbor, head out the front door or to the windows on the third floor to watch them go by. At times, the Livery feels like a community gathering place with political meetings, movies, yoga, lectures, and Community Supported Agriculture drop-offs. The hand-forged micro-brews aren't bad either!

Directions: From I-94, take exit 33, I-94 Business/E Main St. Travel 3.1 miles, then turn left on 5th St. The Livery will be on your left.

Luisa's Cafe

13689 Red Arrow Highway
Harbert, MI 49115
269-469-9037
www.harbertswedishbakery.com

Wednesday - Monday 8 am - 3 pm
Closed Tuesday in summer, closed Tuesday and Wednesday rest of year.

For a comfortable and relaxed Sunday morning brunch, with distinct Scandinavian taste, freshly squeezed orange juice, and natural, mostly organic ingredients, including their specialty buckwheat pancakes, Luisa's is the place to go. It is also the sort of midpoint place where Chicago weekenders will meet local residents for a brunch. The place is relatively small with a dense table arrangement, which somehow also adds to the cozy atmosphere with the light and wooden decor.

Generally too busy to accept reservations, a short wait for a table is often necessary. There is not really an area to stand and wait, but that is rarely a bother as you can shop for delicious Swedish rolls and your weekend copy of the New York Times from the Swedish Bakery situated in the same building. Some highchairs are available for families coming in with young children. The bathroom is small but clean. You can park in front or in their adjacent parking lot. You can find a place for your car more easily than you may find a table for your party!

Service is generally good, but families with young children should be aware that the delicious Dutch apple pancake takes 25 minutes to cook. Luisa's only accepts cash, but if plastic is all you have handy, you can use the drive-through ATM at the bank just next door.

Directions: From I-94, take exit 12 toward Sawyer. Left at Sawyer Rd, then left onto Red Arrow Highway for 1 1/2 miles. Luisa's will be on your right. The sign out front says "Harbert Swedish Bakery."

Panera Bread

3260 Niles Road
St. Joseph, MI 49085
269-428-0700
www.panerabread.com

Monday - Wednesday 6 am - 9 pm
Thursday - Saturday 6 am - 9:30 pm
Sunday 7 am - 8 pm

The Panera chain gets high marks from families for their kids' menu. We love that the bread is whole grain white, the cheese, yogurt and milk are all organic, and the portions are sized appropriately. Other menu options that kids enjoy are the soups served in bread bowls and the granola parfaits. Adults love the breakfast souffles, sandwiches and pastries. Panera Bread is a popular meeting place, and there are usually lots of people with their laptops, taking advantage of the free WiFi while they sip a latte. Allergy information for each menu item is available from the manager or on their website.

Directions: From I-94, take exit 27, heading away from St. Joesph on Niles Rd. Panera Bread is in a shopping center visible from the highway overpass.

The Phoenix

124 Water Street
Benton Harbor, MI 49022
269-925-8060
www.thephoenixbh.com

Monday -Friday 7 am - 4 pm
Saturday 7 am - 1:30 pm

If you are looking for a delicious, healthy and homemade breakfast or lunch, go no further than The Phoenix cafe and coffee shop in the Benton Harbor Arts District. Owner and pastry chef Elizabeth Frost bakes delicious scones, croissants, and other tasty treats. Breakfast offerings also include fresh yogurt with fruit and the best granola ever, and huge yummy breakfast sandwiches. Lunches offer a wide variety of interesting sandwiches, salads, and daily homemade soups. Their sandwiches are made with bread from Zingerman's in Ann Arbor. If you need to order something from Zingerman's, ask if you can order through them.

The Phoenix (cont.)

The Phoenix is bright and open and has both traditional table and chairs, as well as comfy easy chairs and coffee tables. Free wi-fi is available and the cafe is a popular local gathering spot. It is frequently filled with business people having a morning meeting, as well as moms out with their kids for a coffee and a chat. Bathrooms are large and clean. Art from local artists hangs on the walls and is available for purchase.

Directions: From downtown St. Joseph, turn onto Ship St, then make a left on Wayne St to cross over the River. Wayne St becomes Main St as you enter Benton Harbor. Turn right on Pipestone; the Phoenix will be on your left.

Riverfront Cafe

219 N. Front St.
Niles, MI 49120
269-684-2233
www.nilesriverfrontcafe.net

Monday - Thursday 11 am - 9 pm
Friday and Saturday 11 am - 11 pm
Sunday 10:30 am - 2:30 pm

If you're in need of an excellent lunch or dinner in Niles, check out the Riverfront Cafe. Now under new management, this delightful restaurant focuses on fresh and local ingredients of excellent quality. The restaurant is beautiful, with exposed brickwork, oak beams, and a soaring ceiling. They have a list of over twenty sandwiches, as well as salads and soups. We love the house salad, made with mixed baby greens, bleu cheese, spiced almonds and dried cranberries. The kids' menu is pretty standard, but includes a few non-fried options. Applesauce and veggies sticks are offered sides, and kids get crayons and paper to keep them busy while they wait. The dessert plate offers small treats for $2 each; these are impeccably made and usually include a selection of truffles from Veni's Chocolate Shop. This is a great place to grab lunch after enjoying nearby Riverfront Park in the morning.

Directions: From US-31, take exit 5, Niles-Buchanan Rd, towards Niles. Follow the road into town, where it becomes Grant St. Turn left on Lincoln Ave, then right on W Main St and cross the river. Make the first left at Old US-31; the Riverfront Cafe will be on your right. There is a public parking lot directly across the street, on your left.

El Rodeo

1363 Mall Drive
Benton Harbor, MI 49022
269-925-9607
www.elrodeorestaurants.com

Monday - Thursday 11 am - 10 pm
Friday - Saturday 11 am - 10:30 pm
Sunday 11:30 am - 9 pm

If you're looking for a great kid-friendly Mexican restaurant, try El Rodeo. The food is authentic, the waiters are friendly, and the atmosphere is casual and relaxed. They have a good selection of inexpensive kids' meals, such as quesadillas, tacos and enchiladas. On birthdays, they bring out a gigantic sombrero to place on the head of the birthday girl or boy, sing in Spanish and bring sweet fried ice cream with whipped cream. The waiters are happy to allow Americans to practice their Spanish, and Brookview students often order and converse with the waiters in Spanish.

One of the amazing things about El Rodeo is the unbelievable number of plates of food that the waiters are able to balance on their arms at once. It is really pretty remarkable! Favorite meals include carnitas, really flavorful moist shredded pork on your choice of corn or flour tortillas, served with avocado, pico de gallo, rice and beans and tomatillo sauce. We also love nachos al carbon, consisting of tortilla chips with lettuce, tomato, and a mixed grill of beef, chicken and shrimp, topped with a really creamy cheese sauce. The pollo asado (roasted chicken) is also very good. El Rodeo offers several delicious vegetarian options as well, and they serve wine, beer and liquor.

There is a diaper changing station in the bathroom.

Directions: From I-94, take exit 29, Pipestone Rd, towards the mall. Take the first left onto Mall Dr, then take a right as Mall Dr bends. El Rodeo will be on your right.

Roxy's Hamburgers

2629 Cleveland Ave
St Joseph, MI 49085
269-983-1172

Monday - Wednesday 11 am - 4 pm
Thursday - Saturday 11 am - 8 pm

Sometimes, only a good old-fashioned hamburger will do. When the craving strikes, pack up the kids and head to Roxy's Hamburgers, right next to Saint Joseph High School. The teal-and purple building with the winking stoplight and neon "Roxy's" sign is easy to spot. Inside, kids will enjoy the nifty Fifties decor, including lots of posters and album covers featuring pop bands and movie stars from the good old days. There's a big Wurlitzer jukebox loaded with real 45's to keep the mood music playing. If you grab a booth, you'll have fun flipping through the song selectors. However, you're likely to lose your quarters there. If you want to play a song, have the kids go to the main jukebox. They'll want to watch it spring into action as it grabs your record and starts it spinning. The dining room is walled off from the order counter by a glass cabinet full of cars. As you wait for your order, challenge kids to find certain colors or models.

The burgers are cooked to order at Roxy's. Place your order at the counter and take a ticket; then wait for your number to be called. Highlights of the menu include the Roxy Deluxe, which features chopped green olives and mayonnaise in addition to the more pedestrian lettuce and tomato. Roxy's makes a terrific grilled cheese sandwich by using a hamburger bun turned inside out instead of bread. The fries are standard, but the onion rings are wonderful. Kids' meals options include applesauce and milk as healthier alternatives to fries and soda. We love that most of the counter staff knows to offer the options quietly to the parents, in order to prevent pouting from disappointed children.

Outdoor patio seating is available in the warmer months. Roxy's is a popular option when the St. Joe Bears are playing football, as they are located right next to the stadium. Roxy's shares a parking lot with Kelley's Bowl Bowling Alley; the lot is so large it is used as a bus stop for the Krasl Art Fair on the Bluff. Except during local holidays and events, there is plenty of parking.

Directions: From I-94, take exit 27, Niles Ave, heading north. Turn left on Hilltop Ave, then right on Cleveland Ave. Roxy's will be on your right.

Silver Beach Pizza

410 Vine Street
St. Joseph, MI 49085
269-983-4743
www.silverbeachpizza.com

Memorial Day-Labor Day:
Sunday - Thursday noon to 10 pm
Friday and Saturday noon to 11 pm
Winter hours:
Monday - Thursday 4 pm - 9 pm
Friday 4 pm - 10 pm
Saurday noon - 10 pm
Sunday noon - 9 pm

Grab the kids and head downtown to Silver Beach Pizza. The restaurant is located in the train depot at the railroad tracks, just a short walk from Silver Beach. Lines can get long if the beach has been crowded; fortunately, there's a very popular takeout option as well. The restaurant has a wonderful view of the beach and the Whirlpool Compass fountain from the outdoor seating, and there's a whimsical mural of the Silver Beach scene. Inside, there are comfortable booths, and tables big enough for large parties. Take some time to look over the menu, which has some interesting information and photographs about the history of Silver Beach. Kids really enjoy playing with balls of pizza dough and watching the trains while waiting for the real pizza to arrive. Because the pizzas are cooked to order, waiting can be hard on hungry kids. Consider ordering an appetizer, since the kids' meals usually arrive along with the pizza. However, the food, drink, and friendly staff make it worth the wait.

Tim's Too

511 Pleasant Street
St. Joseph, MI 49085
269-985-0094
www.timstoo.com

Monday - Thursday 11 am - 9 pm
Friday - Saturday 11 am - 10 pm

If you are looking for a chance to have some great Mongolian BBQ, then Tim's Too is the place to go! Mongolian BBQ lets you make your own Asian stir-fry, which is cooked on a huge flat-top griddle. First, fill your bowl with your

Tim's Too (cont.)

choice of the huge variety of vegetables and noodles available, then ladle sauces on top to season your dish. Sauces range from curries to teriyaki to spicy Latin-flavored offerings to sesame, ginger and garlic. There are so many options it can be hard to choose! Fortunately, the knowledgeable staff is more than eager to help if you aren't sure. Menus at each table suggest particularly good combinations. Next, you choose a protein like chicken, beef, pork or fish, and finally you decide whether you want your dish to be served as a traditional stir-fry or as a soup or salad. Complimentary flat bread is served, if requested, and both white and brown rice are available. Tim's Too also has some appetizers and desserts on a separate small menu.

The restaurant is small and can be quite noisy and crowded during busy lunchtime hours, but is still a great option for families. Because you choose your own ingredients, it is easy to create a dish that your child will enjoy. We suggest piling the veggies and noodles very high in the bowl, because they cook down substantially on the grill. Also, use at least three ladles of sauce (they're small) to avoid a bland-tasting dish.

Tulips Asian Bistro and Metropolitan Market

3620 Niles Ave
St. Joseph, MI 49085
269-428-8088
www.tulipsbistro.com

Monday - Saturday 11 am - 9 pm
Sunday noon - 8 pm

Tulips is one of the newer restaurants on the Saint Joseph scene, brought to you by the team behind Port 412. The restaurant is attractive and informal, with peaceful green walls, dark wood tables, cement floors, and original art by local artists. The menu focuses on Asian fusion cuisine, with influences from Thailand, Vietnam, Korea, Malaysia and Japan. Their noodle dishes are warm and filling; you can choose to add chicken, tofu or shrimp to make a more complete meal. This is not the place to expect an authentic pad thai, but the chef does load in lots of flavors like lime, chili and cilantro. Tulips also offers popular stir frys, seasoned burgers, and lots of little tasty appetizers. The kid's menu incluldes plain noodles, and the fresh fruit that comes with each choice is one of the best kid's offerings in town. Tulips' takeout is easy and fast, with most orders ready in fifteen minutes. Make sure to check that they've included

Tulips Asian Bistro and Metropolitan Market (cont.)

the fruit if you've ordered a kids' meal to go.

One side of Tulips holds the Metropolitan Market. Definitely get on their Facebook page and email list for the weekly specials from Chef Cameron. The market offers some premade appetizers such as potstickers and crabcakes. They specialize in fresh seafood and beef, frequently getting in supplies of Caribbean grouper, sea scallops, fresh salmon, stone crab claws and more. They will cut your steaks to order right off the hindquarter, and trim them nicely. You can also get fresh mozzarella, real Parmesan and other specialty items. There is a small selection of Asian ingredients, but if you're looking for supplies to complete a recipe, you may need to visit one of the Asian markets in the county.

There is a parking lot right by the door, although it can get crowded at the lunch rush. Spaces are usually open at the far end, away from Panera. The bathrooms are large. There are no changing tables; you could fit a stroller in the handicapped stalls.

Directions: Exit 27 of I-94, heading south. Tulips is in the complex of buildings immediately off the exit, down from Panera Bread.

INTRODUCTION

Slow Snack is a program developed by a group of Brookview parents, which draws inspiration from the international Slow Food movement. Slow Food is a reaction against fast food, and thus stresses healthy, natural, local, sustainable food and food systems. Brookview families preserve produce picked fresh from local orchards and the school's garden to be used as snack ingredients throughout the winter. The entire school practices composting and recycling, finding lessons in the care of our larger environment. The Slow Snack program at Brookview incorporates the Montessori philosophies of grace and courtesy in their shared meal, respect for nature by the content of the snack, and the sense of community by harvesting, processing and cooking together. Our Slow Snack kitchen and garden program is becoming a local model for schools to engage children in raising and preparing food that nourishes while teaching sustainability, civic engagement, and appreciation for the natural environment. The wonderful farms described in this chapter are some of our favorite resources for fresh, local food.

The Blueberry Patch

Holloway Drive
Sawyer, MI 49125
Business Phone: 269-426-4521
Evenings: 269-545-8125

Open mid-July through Labor Day 10 am- 6 pm

One of the best things about Michigan in the summer is the fruit - especially the blueberries. Let's face it: blueberries are one of the things in life that you just can't get enough of AND they're good for you! Every year around the end of July we head to the Blueberry Patch to pick huge quantities of blueberries. The farm will lend you a bucket with a rope loop attached to wear around your neck like a giant necklace to fill with as many ripe blueberries as you can. There are rows and rows of blueberry bushes, and children love discovering bush after bush heavy with ripe fruit. Going early in the day will help you to avoid the heat and the mosquitoes. There are cups of water available, and there is a picnic area in case you want to pack a snack.

If picking blueberries becomes too tedious for you, you can purchase blueberries that they have picked that morning at a slightly higher price per pound.

The Blueberry Patch (cont.)

You can even call ahead and place an order and they will have your blueberries ready for you. We always buy enough to bake some pies or cobbler, to eat plain (or on top of granola), with plenty left over to freeze for the winter. They will pour the berries into a sturdy plastic bag for you to take home, but don't freeze it in the bag or you will wind up with one solid blueberry brick. Pour the berries onto a cookie sheet in a single layer and stick the cookie sheet in the freezer so that the berries freeze individually. Then pour the frozen blueberries into a container or ziplock bag for storage in the freezer. This method allows you to easily pour out as many blueberries as you need on a winter Sunday morning for blueberry pancakes!

If you're looking for a special gift, the Blueberry Patch also sells all kind of things made from blueberries: blueberry jams and jellies, blueberry syrup, blueberry soap, recipe books for things to make with blueberries, and honey from bees who take their nectar from blueberry blossoms!

You will find weekends to be a bit more crowded, but you will have the benefit of the incredible corn-on-the-cob. The farm has crock pots filled with hot water, with a thick layer of butter floating on the top for you to dunk your corn. Stand there and eat it on the spot. It is as messy as it sounds and unbelievably delicious!

Directions: Take I-94 to exit 12, Sawyer, and go west toward Red Arrow Highway. Cross the highway (you are driving toward the lake) and follow the signs on the dirt road about one mile to the farm.

Bredeweg Acres

2268 W. Rockey Weed Road
Stevensville, MI 49127
269-422-2731

Winter: Day after Thanksgiving to December 23
Summer: July and August
Monday - Saturday 10 am - 6 pm
Sunday noon - 6 pm

This is a delightful Christmas Tree and blueberry farm on the outskirts of Stevensville. The nice thing about this farm, besides its convenient location, is its service. The staff is always very helpful and friendly.

Bredeweg Acres (cont.)

During the holiday season you can come and cut your own tree from a variety of different types, including Colorado Blue Spruce, Douglas and Fraser Fir, and Scotch and White Pine. You can pick your own tree from the field and cut it yourself, or you can choose from a selection of pre-cut ones. It doesn't take much time to cut a tree, and if you have family with you, it is always fun to walk in the fields and choose the best tree for your home. If you decide to cut it yourself, the staff is always available to drill the bottom of the tree for a stand, shake, and wrap it for free. However, the part of this whole process our kids enjoy the most is the gift shop. The gift shop is a small hut by the farm house, behind the place where the drilling, shaking, and wrapping takes place. Kids love to pick out a holiday stuffed animal or special handmade ornament for the tree. The shop also offers wreaths. For the holiday season, they are open the day after Thanksgiving until December 23.

The farm is open for blueberries in July and August. Call ahead to be placed on their mailing list, and you'll receive a postcard letting you know when the berries are ready for picking. You can pick yourself or buy their pre-picked boxes. You don't have to take a pail or a bucket - Bredeweg Acres provides tin cans to tie around your waist for use as your picking container! The kids love to go and pick berries and "fill" their own buckets and tummies in the process. You can eat while you pick and they only charge for the blueberries that end up in the bucket. You pay by the weight and the price is reasonable. The trick is to go during the right time when the blueberries are ripe and still on the branches that are easy to pick. But if August comes, life happens, and the calendar gets away from you, and you still want to take the kids blueberry picking, don't panic. Even at the end of the season you can find blueberries if you look at the end of the rows of bushes. Usually the first comers of the season pick from the bushes they first encounter, but if you walk a little until the end of the rows you are almost certain to fill your bucket. Bring a picnic along to make a day of the outing. There is a picnic area and bathroom available. Bredeweg Acres accepts cash and checks only; no credit cards.

Directions: From I-94, take exit 22, John Beers Rd toward Stevensville. Make a right on St. Joseph Ave, which quickly becomes the Stevensville-Baroda Rd. Take a left on Rockey Weed Rd. The farm is about 1/4 mile down the road.

Dinges' Fall Harvest

15219 Mill Road
Three Oaks, MI 49128
269-426-4034
www.harborcountry.com/guide/dingesfarm

Open daily until dark, September and October
Activities open 11 am - 6 pm

Dinges' Fall Harvest has been operated on the family farm of LeRoy and Elaine Dinges since 1973. What originally began as a way to offer the family's pumpkins, gourds and other bounty to the community during the months of September and October has now blossomed into an extravaganza of autumn fun!

The farm has an enormous selection of pumpkins that are cleaned and sorted by size, variety and price. For the more adventurous, head out to the fields and pick your own right off the vine. In addition to the pumpkins, there is a huge selection of gourds, squash, Indian corn and concord grapes to name just a few. Also available are refreshements including hot and cold apple cider, juice, soda, water, coffee, hot chocolate, popcorn, taffy apples, and candy.

However, the fun does not stop there. In addition to the produce, the farm is also home to a variety of activities for kids and kids at heart. There is an educational corn maze, haunted house, pumpkin bounce jumper, tractor rides into the fields, pony rides, giant playhouse pumpkin, bunnies, peacocks and a picnic area with fire pit, to name just a sampling of the fun. Halloween décor is visible throughout the entire grounds, farmhouse and barns.

There is ample parking adjacent to and across the street from the farm, although the grassed lots can get muddy depending on the weather. There are plenty of wagons and wheelbarrows to assist you with transporting your goodies to the car. Cash is the preferred form of payment; credit cards are not accepted. Restrooms are available on-site. Weekends at Dinges are very popular with tourists and weekenders and can be extremely busy. If possible, take the kids after school on a weekday and have the place to yourself.

Directions: Take I-94 to exit 6, Union Pier; turn east onto Elm Valley Rd. Make a left onto Lakeside Rd, followed by a right on Warren Woods Rd. Travel approximately five miles to Mill Rd and make a left. Dinges' is the first house on the right.

Grandpa's Cider Mill

2941 Friday Road
Coloma, MI 49038
269-468-3700
www.grandpascidermill.com

Open daily 9:30 am - 5:30 pm

When you enter Grandpa's Cider Mill, the first thing you see is the actual cider press room, enclosed for your viewing pleasure behind a fifty foot-long glass wall. The apples first go through the washer, then the hopper carries them to the grinder, where they are reduced to mush. One of the workers handles a wide hose that feeds the apple mush into the cider press. This contraption looks a lot like a giant accordian; it slowly squeezes shut and fresh cider flows out the bottom. The bottler is a cool rotating contraption that keeps workers busy changing out full bottles for empty ones. The press starts running Labor Day weekend, and runs Tuesday - Friday during apple season, which usually ends mid-November. If you visit the mill on a day when it's not running, you can still see the machinery, and watch a video of it in action.

The cider bar boasts twenty-five different flavors of cider. Hop on one of the stools at the long blond wood bar and ask for a tasting list. They will be happy to pour you samples. You can try cider flavored with coconut, cantaloupe, maple, spice, ginger, and a whole lot more. Honestly, most of them taste like cider with a bit of additional flavor notes. However, kids really enjoy the anticipation as each flavor is poured, and some of the combinations are surprisingly good. Our favorite was peanut butter cider.

Grandpa's carries preserves, dips and salsas from Jollay Orchards, which is just down the road. They usually have chips and preztels out so you can sample their wares. You can also buy local maple syrup, and some attractive dishes and glasses to serve the goodies you purchase. The bakery counter has fresh doughnuts and apple pies.

Directions: From I-94, take exit 39 (Coloma) onto Friday Rd, heading south. Grandpa's Cider Mill is well marked and is located 0.7 miles down the road, on your left.

Jollay Orchards

1850 Friday Road
Coloma, MI 49038
269-468-3075
www.jollayorchards.com

June - August: Open daily 9:30 am - 5:30 pm
Labor Day - November 1:
Saturday and Sunday 10:30 am-6:30 pm

If it's beautiful weather outside, and you need a change of pace from the beach, check out Jollay Orchards. They have the wonderful fruit for which Berrien County is famous, and they've added enough attractions to keep all the kids in the family happy. Pull into the free parking lot and head inside to the farm market where you will find a bakery with homemade treats and hand-dipped Sherman's ice cream - the cider doughnuts are especially yummy. Next to the farm market is a picnic area with tables and charcoal grills. Jollay Orchards is a great place for the kids to experience picking their own fruit including sweet and tart (pie) cherries, black and red raspberries, peaches, several variety of apples and pumpkins. The picking season generally starts in July, but check out their website or call ahead to find out what fruits are in season. In addition to fruit picking, Jollay Orchards has a playground, small petting zoo, inflatable climbing structures, and plenty of room for kids to burn off some energy.

During the fall "harvest festival," travel by hayride to the apple orchard, pumpkin patch and haunted house. The haunted house is staged inside an old brick house on the edge of the property, and is suitable for kids six and up. You can get on and off for the various attractions at your leisure, as hay wagons come by every 10 minutes. There are often live music events during the festival, which are casual and kid-friendly. The Jollay Orchards pond fishing also is a wonderful place for children to learn the art of fishing. It is a catch-and-release pond where little ones can fish for fifteen minutes or all day. Poles and bait are provided.

Admission is $3.50 for those between the ages of 2 and 65 in the summer and $6 during fall weekends (the farm market and parking are free). Jollay Orchards allows dogs (weekdays only) during the summer as long as they are on a leash.

Directions: From I-94, take exit 39, Millburg/Coloma, heading south on Friday Rd. Jollay Orchards is 1.9 miles down the road, on your right. It is well-marked with a sign.

Lavender Hill Farm

1219 Morris Drive
Niles, MI 49120
269-684-4305
www.thelavenderhill.com

Mid-June - mid-July
Monday - Saturday 9 am - 2 pm

Are you crazy for lavender? Then Lavender Hill Farm is the perfect place to go! During the u-pick season (check on their website) you can go and pick lavender flowers yourself. At their farm store, you can find soap, lavender water (great scent for ironing linen), lavender oil and much more. Check out the yummy lavender-based recipes on their website. Lavender Hill Farm also sets up booths at the Niles French Market if you are looking for their products outside of shop hours. In the off season, they are usually open once or twice a month. You can call and make an appointment if the store isn't open when you need it.

In addition to the lavender, they raise sheep and honeybees, and they have started growing black currants and raspberries.

Directions: US-31 to Exit 5. Go east on Niles-Buchanan Rd. about 1/4 miles and take the first left (Morris Dr). In less than a mile, the farm is on the right side of the road. The shop is around the back of the house.

Lemon Creek Winery and Fruit Farm

533 East Lemon Creek Road
Berrien Springs, MI 49103
269-471-1321
www.lemoncreekwinery.com

November - April: Open daily noon - 5 pm
May - October: Monday - Saturday 10 am - 6 pm
Sunday noon - 6 pm

Lemon Creek Winery and Fruit Farm is a great place to pick or purchase fruit. The adults in your party will also appreciate the chance to taste a full range of wines. The Lemon Family has 150 years of grape and fruit growing experience in Berrien County. The farm offers some of the broadest fruit selection

Lemon Creek Winery and Fruit Farm (cont.)

around, including both wine and table grapes, nectarines, apricots, sweet cherries, apples and plums. The winery is quaint and you will find a range of wines, including ice wines. Lemon Creek hosts events from car shows to art and musical festivals. Although they are a winery, they go out of their way to make these festivals kid-friendly, including games and activities. Most events include food from their own outdoor kitchen, and you are welcome to bring a picnic of your own. Outside wine and spirits are not permitted.

Directions: From I-94, take exit 27, Niles Rd, heading south. Quickly veer right onto Hollywood Rd at the traffic light. Travel 6.9 miles on Hollywood Rd; Lemon Creek Winery and Fruit Farm will be on your left.

Nye's Apple Barn

3151 Niles Road
St. Joseph, MI 49085
269-429-0596
www.nyesapplebarn.com

Open May - October
9 am - 6 pm
Limited hours at the beginning and end of the season; call ahead.

Nye's Apple Barn is a standout among farm stands for several reasons. First of all, it's very conveniently located, just off Exit 27 on busy Niles Avenue. It's easy to make a quick stop for fresh fruits and vegetables on your way home from school or work. Secondly, they take both credit and debit cards, an innovation we wish more farms could introduce. Finally, in addition to their produce, they carry jams, jellies, flower planters, maple syrup, honey, and a wide range of preserves.

The Barn offers freshly picked fruits and vegetables. In the early part of the growing season, some of the items are not local, which may save you a trip to the grocery store to pick up those last few ingredients. Nye's also runs a U-Pic option; berries, grapes, and cherries can be picked at the Barn, while peaches and apples are picked down the road at the family farm. Small baskets are provided for the berries at no charge; bushel baskets and bags for the apples cost a small amount. Nye's has a wide range of apple varieties, and the staff at the farm can help you choose the right kinds based on your plans.

Nye's Apple Barn (cont.)

We love the Empire apples for baking. The minimum purchase is one bushel, so you may want to make plans to share with another family.

Nye's ships their apples all over the country in gift boxes. They will pack the apples in trays or in foam to ensure maximum protection. The Honey Crisp apple is a relatively new variety and would be a treat for an apple lover in another part of the country that hasn't had a chance to try it yet. October and early November are prime months for apple boxes, since the apples are at the peak of their flavor.

Directions: From I-94, take exit 27, Niles Ave, towards St. Joseph. Nye's is easily visible almost immediately, on your right.

Pinecrest Christmas Tree Farm

4403 Spring Creek Road
Galien, MI 49113
269-545-8125

Open in season daily 9 am - 6 pm

If you like to chop down your own Christmas tree, Pinecrest is a great place to go. Horse-drawn hayrides pick guests up every ten minutes or so. The wagons can hold ten to twelve people each. If your little one wants to sit up front with the driver, just ask. Our four-year-old asked, "Who sits up there," and she was quickly invited to sit in a place of honor with the best view. Once you're situated, whether it's with the driver or comfortably on bales of hay, it's only another ten minutes until you're out among hundreds of trees. They have a variety of balsams, pines, firs, and spruces to choose from. They even provide a saw. Your only decision is which of the hundreds of perfect Christmas trees is your tree. Once you have chosen and chopped it down, simply drag it to the main path to be picked up by another horse-drawn hayride to be taken back. They also have a tractor that pulls a larger wagon to accommodate even more people.

The customer service is wonderfully friendly. Your tree will have all its loose needles shaken free, then it will be wrapped and tied to the top of your car. Inside the main building is a good selection of Christmas ornaments. They also have concessions like cotton candy and free hot chocolate. There are also crayons and coloring pages for the little ones.

Pinecrest Christmas Tree Farm (cont.)

Directions: From I-94, take exit 4A, Pulaski Highway/US-12 E towards Niles. After about 5 miles, make a right onto S Elm St, which soon becomes 3 Oaks Rd. Veer left to stay on 3 Oaks Rd as it splits, then take the second left onto W Spring Creek Rd. Pinecrest Christmas Tree Farm will be on your left.

Stover's Farm Market

7837 M-139
Berrien Springs, MI 49103
269-471-1401
www.stoversupic.com

Open May - November, depending on growing conditions
Monday - Saturday, 9 am - 6 pm
Closed Sundays

You can't miss the big red barn driving down M-139 with "Stover's" on the roof. More than a site for a great farm market, the building is a piece of local history. It was built in 1865 using wooden pegs instead of nails. The 50-foot long crossbeams are hand-hewn. The barn was moved about three miles to its present location in 1990. Antique farm implements are on display inside and a whiteboard in the front of the barn describes the history of this fantastic structure. Kids find it fascinating to read about and imagine life on the farm over a hundred years ago. Friendly cats snooze in the sun at the entrance.

The Stover family represents five generations of farmers in the area. They open each year in May when the asparagus ripens, and close in November with the last of the apples. In between, they offer a huge variety of fruits, many available for U-Pic as well as for pre-picked purchase. In June, they have strawberries, sweet and tart cherries, and red and black raspberries. July and August bring over thirty varieties of peaches, as well as blackberries, blueberries and apricots. Heading into the fall months, there are apples, grapes, pumpkins and late raspberries. There are also vegetable crops available throughout the growing season, such as tomatoes, peppers, and some vividly colored purple cauliflower.

There are many products available for sale in the barn. Stover's has their own line of canned goods, including a huge selection of jams and jellies, pickles, relishes, and salsas. There are also sugar-free products. They sell honey,

Stover's Farm Market (cont.)

including raw and comb forms, in containers as large as five pounds. Stover's has a small cider press and they treat their cider with UV sterilization instead of pasteurization, which makes for a fresher tasting cider. You can also buy soaps and lotions made with goat's milk, maple syrup, scented candles, caramel apples, and handmade candy treats such as chocolate- coated pretzel sticks. One wall has a selection of wonderful model trucks and cars in polished wood, almost too pretty to be toys.

To pick your own produce, stop by the barn first to sign up and get directions to the particular area where you'll be picking. Some of the orchards are a short drive down M-139, no more than five minutes. The orchards have picnic tables so you can pack a lunch and take a break. The folks at the barn will tell you what crops are best at the moment. Stover's provides containers for your pickings at no extra charge. They welcome children, but those under ten require supervision. Stover's takes credit cards.

Directions: From US-31, take exit 15, MI-139, towards Benton Harbor. Travel 1.8 miles; Stover's will be on your right.

Tree-Mendus Fruit Farm

9351 E. Eureka Rd.
Eau Claire, MI 49111
269-782-7101
www.treemendus-fruit.com

June through Labor Day:
Open daily 10 am - 6 pm
Closed Tuesdays
Labor Day - October:
Friday - Monday 10 am - 6 pm
November - mid-December:
Country Market open Monday - Friday 10 am - 2 pm

The Tree-Mendus Fruit Farm is located on 450 acres in the center of Berrien County. This family-run farm grows over 200 varieties of apples, as well as cherries, peaches, plums, pears and more. The Heritage Apple collection is a unique feature of this farm. Where else can you sample the Calville Blanc D'hiver, favored as a dessert apple in France, the Esopus Spitzenberg, favorite apple of Thomas Jefferson, and many others?

Tree-Mendus Fruit Farm (cont.)

There are several choices to let you purchase the fruit you want. During the summer, call ahead to the "Ripe-N-Ready Report" to find out what's best, then drop in for a U-Pic session. More dedicated apple eaters have the chance to rent their personal tree, located in a private orchard on farm grounds. The staff performs the maintenance, but the harvesting is done by your family. Finally, those without the time and inclination to pick their own fruit can always purchase some at the country store. They have samples available so you can find the right fruit for your tastes. The store also carries farm products, including their Cherry Brite topping, and local Michigan honey and maple syrup.

Tree-Mendus Fruit Farm hosts the International Cherry Pit Spitting competition, where the Guiness-recognized record holders are crowned. Generally held on July 4th, the qualifying round is open to everyone and divided into age brackets. Repeat champions have travelled many miles to return to the farm each year to defend their title. On summer weekends, the farm offers pony rides in the afternoons, and wagons to carry you to the U-Pic spots in the orchard. Picnic areas and playgrounds are available. Larger groups can reserve the covered picnic pavilions, including a country-cooked chicken dinner. The guided tours of the orchard have been a Brookview favorite in years past, and can be booked by school groups. Highlights include an apple tree that has been grafted to grow twenty different types of apples. Kids also enjoy seeing widely different apple varieties, in many different shapes and colors.

Directions: From I-94, take exit 29 (Pipestone Rd). Merge onto Meadowbrok Rd, go 8 miles, turn right on MI-140 S and go 5.5 miles. Turn left on E. Eureka Rd.

INTRODUCTION

Outdoor education is a high priority in Montessori education. At Brookview, there is a beautiful boardwalk path through the woods, which leads to our prairie on the Saint Joseph River. Whenever possible, teachers take children out to the prairie to study biology, zoology, and for older children, sustainability and environmental issues. Berrien County is fortunate to have an abundance of opportunities to expose children to nature. An afternoon in the woods is a guaranteed fun family experience, winter, spring, summer, or fall.

Fernwood Botanical Garden

Fernwood Botanical Garden
13988 Range Line Road
Niles, MI 49120-9020
269-695-6491
www.fernwoodbotanical.org

May - October: Tuesday - Saturday 10 am - 6 pm
Sunday noon - 5 pm
November - April: Tuesday - Saturday 10 am - 5 pm
Sunday noon - 6 pm

Fernwood Botanical Gardens is a must-see for families in Berrien County. The 105 acre campus borders the St. Joseph river, and is home to both planned gardens and a nature preserve. There is something happening during every season of the year. The grounds are lovely at all times of year, and the paved walks are level and accessible to people with limited mobility. The visitor center holds a cafe that serves soup, panini and gourmet salads for lunch, as well as a gift center where honey and lavender sachets from the Fernwood gardens are particular favorites. The indoor fern garden makes a nice tropical getaway in the middle of winter, and kids especially love the banana trees. Just outside the welcome center are paved walkways that take you past the herb garden (surrounding a traditional English stone dovecote) and a sensory garden that lets you explore all your senses. The Nature Center is staffed by dedicated and friendly naturalists that set up excellent learning opportunities for kids of all ages. You can also check out a living honeybee hive and borrow some binoculars to watch the birds that flock to the feeding station outside the windows.

The nature preserve is an outstanding chance to see several different environ-

Fernwood Botanical Garden (cont.)

ments. Fernwood has reconstructed five acres of tallgrass prairie, which can grow up to twelve feet high by the end of summer. There is also a pond where herons, turtles, and other wildlife gather. Make sure to try one of their wilderness trails in April and May to look for spring wildflowers, including Michigan's endangered trillium. The numerous gardens contain lots of treasures, including a Discovery Garden with hands-on activities for kids, and the Bauer Terrace, planted to attract hummingbirds and butterflies. One special attraction, new to Fernwood in 2009 and now a part of their permanent collection, is the Railway Garden. This is a beautiful outdoor multi-tiered layout with 510' of track, running several different trains. The visible building supports are all of natural materials. Each year, the display buildings will change with a particular theme. Make sure to get one of the pamphlets that list all the special things to find. The Railway garden opens in May and generally runs through the summer, but call ahead to confirm.

There are lots of organized activities for kids and families at Fernwood. They run art and nature camps throughout the summer, and the Nature Center is a favorite destination for field trips. One family favorite is the opportunity to try geocaching. Geocaching (pronounced geo-cashing, like cashing a check) is an outdoor treasure-hunting game. Instead of an old pirate map with an "X" marking the spot, geocachers use Global Positioning System receivers to hide and seek containers called geocaches or simply caches. Caches typically hold "treasure" of inexpensive trinkets, unusual coins, or books. For those new to geocaching, Fernwood will offer 60 minutes of basic skill training and then send you out with seasoned geocachers for your adventure. Necessary gear can be borrowed if you don't have a GPS.

Admission to Fernwood is a bit pricey: $7 for adults, $5 for seniors, $4 for teens, and $3 for kids age 6-12. Consider purchasing a membership, which allows free admission for one year as well as other benefits. A Basic membership covers three people for $40; a Preferred membership covers six people for $60. There is so much to see at Fernwood that your family will want to visit multiple times over the year.

Directions: From US-31 take exit 7, Walton Road, and go west (toward Buchanan) 1.7 miles to Range Line Road. Turn right on Range Line Road and travel 1.7 miles to the Fernwood entrance. Signs from US 31 are easy to follow.

Love Creek Nature Center and Park

9292 Huckleberry Road
Berrien Center, MI 49102
269-471-2617
www.berriencounty.org/parks

The Love Creek Nature Center is located in Love Creek Park. The outstanding feature of this park are the hiking and skiing trails, spread over 150 acres. The trails take you through beech forests, old fields slowly being reclaimed by the forest, Love Creek and its associated marshes. Trails are very well marked, and an easy-to-read trail map, with descriptions of the terrain, is available at the Nature Center. During ski season, the trails are groomed to give you the best conditions for skiing.

At the entrance to the park, with an ample parking lot, sits the attractive stone Nature Center. In the winter, this is the place to purchase ski trail passes and rent skis, then warm up after your outing. In the warmer months, take advantage of the many naturalist programs. There are fitness hikes, birding expeditions, canoe rides, preschooler programs, and more. Details are best found on the website, as they change frequently.

Dogs are not permitted on the trails. When there is snow on the ground, the ski trails are off-limits to hikers, but a dedicated one mile loop remains open at all times. If there's no snow, all the trails allow hikers. Love Creek also features a 4.5 mile mountain bike trail that is good for beginners to intermediate bikers, open spring - fall. Please note that Love Creek takes cash only for entrance fees, ski passes and ski rentals. We recommend calling ahead to see if the center has closed for various activities; you can still use the trails if that's the case, but make sure you have all the equipment and food you need.

Directions: Take US-31 South, through Berrien Springs. Cross over the St. Joseph River and then make a left onto Deans Hill Road. Next, make an immediate right onto Pokagon Road, followed by a right onto Huckleberry Road. Love Creek will be on your left. There are signs at the intersection of Deans Hill and Pokagon, and again at the entrance to the park.

Margaret Upton Arboretum

280 S. Water Street
St. Joseph, MI 49085
269-983-6301

Open year round, no closing times

Whether you are seeking a great view of the boats that head along the St. Joseph river, are looking for a nice picnic location, would like to discover contemporary sculpture, or just want to relax along the water, the Arboretum is a great place. An easy walk from Silver Beach or downtown St. Joseph, the Arboretum provides picnic tables, benches and a paved trail for walking, biking, strollers or scooters. The Krasl Art Center places sculptures along the Arboretum. These change every couple of years. For infomation about the sculptures, stop by the Krasl for a booklet or use your phone to dial the number located on each plaque for more information. Generally speaking it is acceptable to touch outdoor sculptures but these are not considered playthings and children (and adults) should not climb on them.

Whether you enjoy a quiet lunch on a picnic blanket or at one of the picnic tables, look out for feathered friends. They will certainly come visit and beg for treats. Keep your eye on the river. You never know when a barge will pull up across the river to unload materials at Lafarge. You are also likely to see power boats, sail boats, tug boats and maybe the U.S. Coast Guard boat. Keep your ears peeled for trains, this is a great location to watch the train bridge in action.

A couple times a year you will find this park busy for festivals and regattas including the Tri State Regatta and the Venetian Festial.

Please use caution near the river's edge. The railing will not keep unattended young children from tumbling into the water. The closest public restrooms are located at Silver Beach.

Directions: Drive all the way through downtown St. Joseph on State Street. The Margaret Upton Arboretum is just in front of you as the road curves sharply to the left. Parking is available on the right hand side.

Sarett Nature Center

2300 Benton Center Road
Benton Harbor, MI 49022
269-927-4382
www.sarett.com

Trails: Open dawn to dusk daily

Kids love to explore the outdoors year-round at Sarett Nature Center. The main hall has a terrific selection of permanent exhibits, including a number of live animals. The naturalists will allow you to feed the bunnies, and you may get a chance to pet the nine-foot snake! If that's not your cup of tea, try to see Big Red, the little owl who lost an eye in a car accident and now happily lives at Sarett. You can watch birds flock at the feeders outside the windows and touch various natural objects such as snakeskins and wasp nests. There is a library of nature books for young children, a puppet theater, and an indoor sandbox for digging. There are lots of taxidermy specimens of local Michigan fauna.

Sarett's main building was recently expanded, and it is beautiful. Check out the great room, with high ceilings, wood floors, huge windows and a stone fireplace. The main entrance holds a gift shop, and is a terrific place to get high-quality birdseed, birding and garden supplies, toys and local products such as honey. During the spring, Sarett taps their maple trees to produce their own syrup. It's fun to walk through the trails and see the buckets hanging from each tree.

Outside, nature trails wind through the woods, wetlands, and prairies. The Treetop Walkway is not to be missed! This incredible platform takes you far out over a ravine; walnut and elm trees rub against the railings and creak in the wind. The view from the end of the platform is wonderful. The railings are very secure; children may be scared by the heights, but there's no possible way from them to slip through and fall. Sarett's trails are open for cross country skiing in the winter. Skis are available to rent for an additional fee.

Sarett offers nature classes for ages three and up during the summer; members receive a discount. Sign up early, because these day classes tend to fill up quickly. Younger children focus on a single animal in their class, and usually do an imaginative craft. Older kids have a chance to learn kayaking or canoing, go fossil hunting, learn geocaching, or muck through a marsh. Birthday parties at Sarett are a terrific deal. The facility is beautiful and the great room

Sarett Nature Center (cont.)

has a full kitchen attached to it. The naturalists will bring out some live animals and do a little talk. There are so many great activities for families here; we highly recommend a membership. Admission for non-members is $3 per person for those over 12; a family membership is $40 and gets you in free for a year.

Directions: Take I-94 to 196-N. Take Exit 1, Red Arrow Highway. Turn left and travel 1/8 of a mile on Benton Center Rd. Turn right and proceed 3/4 of a mile. The Nature Center is on the left and is marked with a sign.

INTRODUCTION

Brookview families tend to really enjoy the great outdoors, and this chapter of the Guide grew the fastest as everyone contributed their favorite getaways. We love the parks where kids can invent their own games, run around, get dirty, and hopefully get themselves thoroughly tired. The outdoor spaces on Brookview's campus are as well-used and loved as the indoor ones. Primary students head outdoors in all but the coldest winter weather to stretch their legs. Part of the playground is home to our two sheep; feeding and watering them are the responsibility of all the classrooms in turn. We grow vegetables for our school snack in another corner of the playground. Behind the school, a boardwalk path through the forest allows Elementary students the chance to pursue nature studies and develop their own research topics. This chapter offers the chance to sample some of the wonderful beauty of Berrien County's natural heritage. Have fun!

Bicentennial Park

Corner of E. John Beers and Scottdale Roads
St. Joseph, MI 49085
269-429-2501
www.royaltontownship.org
Open daily, dawn - dusk

This is a small playground tucked behind the volunteer fire station on John Beers Road. The shelter holds twelve picnic tables. Royalton Township residents can reserve the park and gain access to the service building, which holds a fridge and oven. There is no sink, but there is a water faucet on the outside of the building. A food-serving window allows the cooking area communication with the shelter. The building also holds bathrooms. In the warmer months, porta-potties are present for times when the shelter building is not open. To reserve the park, residents can show up in person at the township office (980 Miners Road, St. Joseph) on the first Monday in April - this is the recommended procedure if there is a particular date required. Telephone reservations can be made starting in May. There is a dumpster in the parking lot, and those who have reserved the park will be allowed to leave trash there at the end of the day.

Bicentennial Park (cont.)

The playground consists of swings, old-fashioned teeter-totters, and slides. There is no fence, but the playground is set well back from both roads. There are benches and a few grills scattered around, and some trees provide shade. There is a nice grassy area for running and playing catch. If your needs include more indoor space or a fully equipped kitchen, consider the Tryon School Community Center directly across John Beers Road. This 19th century clapboard schoolhouse now serves as meeting space and can also be rented through the Royalton Township Office.

Directions: From I-94, take Exit 27 South; veer right onto Hollywood Road. Make a right onto E. John Beers Road. Bicentennial Park is at the intersection of Scottdale and John Beers Roads, behind the fire station, on your left.

Carronde Park

2650 Riverbend Drive
Benton Harbor, MI 49022

Open daily, dawn - dusk

Nestled behind a residential area is Carronde Park, a large park located on the St. Joseph River and a great place to spend an afternoon. The park has a number of different playground areas that cater to different aged children. There are large grassy areas and shady treed areas with picnic tables. Bring along rackets and hit a ball around on one of the tennis courts. There is also a boat launch for those who want to get out on the water. Carronde is located across the river from the much larger Riverview Park.

The park is predominantly used by locals; it is well-kept and usually not crowded. It is common to see neighborhood residents walking around the circular drive for a bit of exercise. There are public restrooms, and covered pavilions are available for larger gatherings.

Directions: From I-94, take exit 28, M-139/Scottdale Rd, north towards Benton Harbor. Make a left on Nickerson Ave, followed by a left on Colfax Ave. Colfax bends to the right and becomes Jakway Ave. Make a left on Lu-Al Dr. and another left on Riverbend Dr. The park will be on your left.

FOP Sports Park

3470 Angling Road
Coloma, MI 49038

Open year-round 8 am - 10 pm

The FOP Sports Park in Coloma hosts AYSO games as well as baseball games on its many playing fields. Spectators can watch from the bleachers, or retreat to the two picnic pavilions to get some shade. Younger children will enjoy the cheerful yellow and green play structure, resting on a mulch base, with tall slides, monkey bars, and climbing towers. The baseball fields have covered dugouts for the players. The large parking lot is dirt and develops ruts quickly, but there are cement walkways to the pavilions and fields, making it easy to wheel along strollers or picnic coolers. There are trash cans and porta-potties available. The pavilions have concession windows open in the warmer months. We love that each window sports two cement steps so that even the youngest child can climb up and place an order.

Directions: I-94 to exit 39; travel south on Friday Road. Make a quick left on Mountain Rd and another left on Angling to pull into the parking lot.

Grand Mere State Park

Stevensville, MI 49127

Open daily, dawn - dusk

Main entrance requires vehicle permit in the summer

Grand Mere State Park includes a mile of Lake Michigan shoreline, sand dunes, forest, and three lakes that were left behind by the retreating glaciers. The main entrance to the park is just off I-94 at exit 22. After a short drive down a gravel road into the woods, you'll come to a parking lot. There are two outhouse style bathrooms, and several nature trails. A picnic shelter is a few hundred feet away. It holds six tables comfortably and has a large grill near it. The trails are well maintained, easy to follow, and have benches placed at wide intervals to rest and admire the view. This part of the park is located between the Middle and South Grand Mere lakes, and the nature trail splits so that you can go around each. Keep heading west, up steep dunes, to get to the undisturbed Lake Michigan beaches. Grand Mere is a popular spot for hiking and

Grand Mere State Park (cont.)

cross country skiing in season. Dogs are welcome on leashes.

Since much of Berrien County is flat, sledding hills are at a premium, and Grand Mere boasts some of the best. The dunes make for terrific sledding. If you go through the main entrance, you will have a fairly long walk through the woods to get to the hills, and many sledding trails are rather narrow. Large groups may want to take walkie-talkies to keep in communication as you scout the best places. For those with smaller kids, we advise using the lesser-known entrance to Grand Mere, between the Middle and North Lakes. Exit 22 off I-94 is Grand Mere Road. If you follow that road all the way to the end, you'll pass Lincoln Township's North Lake Park. Keep going through a residential section and the road will dead-end in a parking lot. On the right is Lincoln Township beach, with a narrow path between private residences to Lake Michigan. On the left, there are signs indicating an entrance to Grand Mere. You need to step between a utility pole and highway fence to get on the path. From there, it's about a quarter mile of flat trail through the woods. Then you're at some prime sledding hills! A large dune faces you as you emerge from the woods - this one is for daredevils only. Follow the trail to your right to "The Bowl." Two dunes face each other with a cleft in between. Sled down the gentle slope between the two dunes for a long and easy ride, or climb to the top of one side for a steeper drop. There are no trees to endanger your sledding runs here.

Grand Mere's beaches are primarily attractive for their remote and private location. There are no amenities such as bathrooms, and the walk can be long and hot. Try to keep gear to a minimum, and be aware that black flies can be aggressive, especially on days when there's an offshore breeze from the Lake. We find there are lots of other Berrien beach options with easier access. Grand Mere is fantastic in the spring, fall and winter. Duck hunting is permitted on the Middle and South lakes. There is a boat launch on Grand Mere Road serving Middle Lake.

Directions: From I-94, take Exit 22, Grand Mere Road, heading west towards Lake Michigan. For the main entrance to Grand Mere State Park, with access to the picnic shelter and bathrooms, make a quick turn onto Thornton Rd heading south, which runs right alongside I-94. The park entrance is well marked on your right a short distance down Thornton.

Harbert Community Park

Red Arrow Highway
Harbert, MI 49115
(Just north of the Chikaming Township Hall at
13535 Red Arrow Highway)
269-469-1676

Open daily 8 am - 10:30 pm

Harbert Community Park is an excellent place for a family picnic or a leisurely afternoon of fun for the kids. The park is located directly off Red Arrow Highway with ample parking. A public restroom is available. There is a pavilion with two grills and 12 picnic tables. Several large trees provide plenty of shade. For the children there are swings, a slide and a climbing structure. Also on site is a small pond containing mostly bluegill. You will need to bring your own equipment if you plan to do any fishing. There is no barrier between the park and the water, so keep a close eye on small children.

Harbert Park used to be home to the local Little League association. The league has since moved to another location, but a regulation size Little League baseball field (including bleachers and a concession stand) is located on the property. While the field is no longer maintained for the purposes of the league, it is still a great spot for practice or a family game.

Chikaming Township has several plans for Harbert Community Park. A fenced dog park, adjacent to the baseball field, is near completion. There have also been plans to add a lighted ice skating rink on the ball field in the winter months. As of publication, these plans were not yet final.

Directions: From I-94, take exit 12, Sawyer Rd., towards Sawyer. Make a left onto Red Arrow Highway. The park will be one mile down Red Arrow Highway, on your left.

Hays Park

Intersection of Main Street and Paw Paw Avenue
Watervliet, MI 49098

Open daily, dawn - dusk

Hays Park (cont.)

Hays Park is a multiuse park and the largest park in Watervliet. There seems to be some confusion about the name - all the online listings we could find call it "Hayes Park" but the sign on Main Street directs you to "Hays Park." When you first enter, you'll encounter the dirt parking lot and the three baseball fields. Each has bleachers and covered dugouts. There's a cinderblock bathroom structure and a drinking fountain. The modern play structure has a good view of the fields, so younger children (the structure is rated ages 5 - 12) can burn off some energy if spectating gets them fidgety. Hays also boasts a skate park, where bicyclists, skateboarders and rollerbladers are welcome to try out the ramps and steps. The park is meant to appeal to all skill levels; protective gear is strongly encouraged. Further back, the park has a canoe launch on to the minute Little Paw Paw River. There is fishing, but the preferred spot seem to be on the other side of the river. Continue along the access road past the skate park and you'll find the picnic pavillion, which holds about twenty picnic tables comfortably. There are a few grill boxes for cooking. This area of the park is low-lying, next to the river, and can get muddy. On slightly higher ground, there's a small hill covered with oaks, with a slide, merry-go-round, and benches. There is more parking at the top of the hill. In the winter, the hill attracts sledders, who whiz down the fairly steep slope into the parking lot below. Drive carefully when entering the park to avoid any mishaps.

Directions: From I-94, take exit 41, heading north on Main Street. Make a right on Paw Paw Avenue; the park is easy to see from Main Street.

Indian Fields Grove Park

End of Cass Street and Main Street
Berrien Springs, Michigan 49103

Open dawn to 11 pm daily

Overlooking beautiful Lake Chapin, Indian Fields Grove Park is a large open space with lots of tall oak trees. This is one of the best parks in Berrien County, but is often overlooked, keeping crowds to a minimum. The highlight is the huge wooden play structure, which has something for kids of all ages. There is a separate toddler section with a sand pit, bucket swings and short slides, as well as low-to-the-ground climbing areas. A small replica downtown, including a court house and fire station, leave room for imaginative play.

Indian Fields Grove Park (cont.)

Older kids will enjoy the two story walkway that offers a terrific view of the lake, as well as longer slides, monkey bars, and tall towers with ladders for quick escapes. Since the park is so big, parents will appreciate that the play structure is separately fenced, so that kids can't wander off. The ground cover is woodchips, and no smoking is permitted in this area of the park.

Two nearby open pavilions comfortably house about six picnic tables each; these can be reserved by Village residents but are otherwise available for general use. There are lots of wonderful places to place a picnic blanket and let your kids run off some steam. The high bluff overlooking the lake is not fenced, but is far away from the play structure. Remnants of an old bridge are still visible at the left side of the sweeping vista. The grounds under the oak trees are hilly enough for young children to enjoy sledding. There is a fence around the entire park, and the nearby streets, which dead-end at the park, are residential and relatively quiet.

A cinderblock building holds restrooms, which are open in the warmer months. There is a water fountain near the play structure. Picnic tables and trashcans are plentiful. There is ample parking.

Directions: From US-31, take exit 15, M-139, through the Village of Berrien Springs, where the road is named Cass Street. Cass Street dead-ends into the park.

Jean Klock Park

Benton Harbor, MI 49022

Open daily, 8 am - 10 pm
$2 charge for parking from Memorial Day - Labor Day

The renovated Jean Klock Park was introduced in 2009. A long, sweeping drive takes you past several holes of the Harbor Shores golf course. Traffic flows around two circles, featuring stunning sculptures in the center. Parking stretches out in long lanes, and no spot is very far from the wide sandy beaches. If you choose to bike to the beach, there are racks to lock your bike. The park offers a great view of the lighthouse; consider it for an alternative viewing spot for the July 4 fireworks. At the center of the park, you'll find public restrooms, with partially enclosed showers to wash off the sand. Jean Klock also boasts

Jean Klock Park (cont.)

a large shaded picnic pavilion, highlighted by decorative mosaics depicting Michigan wildlife. There are picnic grills so you can enjoy a cookout as you watch the waves. The children's play structure is somewhat small, but they do offer a row of swings with fantastic views of the lake.

A wooden walkway takes you up the dunes for a view of the golf course; there's a gazebo at the top of the dunes providing a shady area to rest. A second walkway leads you through beach grass to a small platform for a more quiet, contemplative view of the lake. Jean Klock beach is fantastic - broad and smooth, with plenty of space to stretch out and enjoy the sand. It's a relatively short walk from the parking lot to the water's edge, which families with young toddlers will particularly appreciate.

Locals know that there's been significant controversy surrounding Jean Klock Park recently. However, the beach is absolutely beautiful, and we hope will be enjoyed by families and visitors for many years to come.

Directions: From I-94, take exit 27, MI-63/Niles Rd, heading north. After 3.7 miles, veer to the right as Niles Rd becomes Main St. Cross over the St. Joseph River; turn left onto Klock Rd. Make the first right onto Jean Dr, the the first left onto Park St. Enter Jean Klock Park; follow the road to get to the beach and beach parking.

Kathryn Park

Corner of Moccasin and Fourth Streets
Buchanan, MI 49107

Kathryn Park is a quiet community park in residential Buchanan. The handsome wrought iron archway forms the entrance to the park; two plaques commemorate the "Monday Club" and the "30 Club," both of which contributed to the park's formation in 1941. Scattered under the oak trees is a small selection of playground equipment, including a slide, monkey bars, a sandbox, and swings. One interesting feature is a "log roller" - hold on to the handlebars and try to keep your balance on top of a polished metal cylinder. A stone bench was placed by the International Order of Odd Fellows and their logo of three chain links is replicated several times on the bench. Trash cans are available, and there is a water fountain in the warmer months. There are benches, but no picnic tables.

Kathryn Park (cont.)

The park is not fenced and borders several backyards; the residental streets are relatively quiet. Parking is easiest on Fourth Street, across from the park.

Directions: From US-31, take exit 7, Walton Rd. Cross over the river; the road becomes River St. Veer slightly left onto Red Bud Trail, then take an immediate right onto Fourth St.

Kiwanis Park

St. Joseph, MI 49085
269-983-6341

Open daily, 8 am - 10 pm

Kiwanis Park features a skate park, dog park, basketball court, baseball diamond, picnic pavilion, tennis court, and multi-age playground.

Grab your skateboard, scooter or bike, helmet and kneepads, and hit the fenced-in skate park. Or, just sit on the bench and enjoy the spectacle of risk takers of all ages using this section of the park. The posted schedule suggests specific hours for each wheeled item but this is loosely followed and unenforced. The area is kept quite clean and big kids are usually great about watching out for little kids.

The dog park is frequented by dogs of all sizes. You'll find the spacious, tree-lined and grassy park a great place for dogs to run and play fetch. The two-gate entrance minimizes escapes and the enclosed area even features a drinking fountain for two- and four-legged creatures. To the side is a small-dog park, which is seldom used. The shady lawn and numerous benches make the fenced-in area of the park comfy for humans as well. Families are discouraged from bringing children into the fenced-in area. Even the dogs with the best of intentions can accidently knock over a child while running with other dogs. Visitors often leave extra tennis balls and frisbees and set up a doggie pool in the summer months.

To the far end of the park, you'll find a full basketball court and baseball diamond. Bring your own equipment, or join a game already taking place. The basketball court is frequently used after school. You're very likely to find the baseball diamond vacant.

Kiwanis Park (cont.)

You'll find three distinct playground areas at Kiwanis: pre-school, school-age and old-school. The two modern playground areas are adjacent to one another and close to the picnic pavilion. The sandy surface makes this a great place to bring the beach toys. In the back corner, you'll find a classic, old-school metal playground complete with double decker merry-go-round, swingset and very tall curly slide.

In the winter, you'll find neighborhood children sledding down the access road next to the baseball diamond. The steep path can be great fun, but the very steep cliff on the ravine side (only fenced 1/2 the way down) poses a hazard. Sled at your own risk, as sledding is not suggested by the city.

Additional amenities include drinking fountains, seasonal rest rooms, and a covered pavilion with picnic tables and BBQ pits. Even on the busiest of days, there's room for everyone at this spacious park. A word of warning, as it is located at the bottom of the ravine, all unpaved areas of this park flood after a rainstorm.

Directions: From I-94, take exit 27, M-63/Niles Ave heading north. Take a right onto Napier Ave, the the third left onto Langley Ave. The entrance to Kiwanis Park will be on your left, almost a mile down Langley.

Lake Bluff Park

Along Lake Boulevard
St. Joseph, MI 49085

Lake Bluff Park is a wonderful six-block long park that runs along the bluff on the west side of downtown St. Joseph. This park, overlooking Lake Michigan, is an integral part of downtown St. Joseph. Many events are held at Lake Bluff Park, including the Krasl Art Fair, Antiques on the Bluff, Chalk the Block, and many more.

During the summer, it is a great place to take a stroll and enjoy the beautiful view. There are a number of memorials and sculptures along the park, and there are also picnic tables, benches, and swings, which provide nice spots to take a break and relax. In the winter, the park is lit up with many lights and is a great place to go for a walk on a crisp evening.

The park has public restrooms available at the staircase (located at Lake

Lake Bluff Park (cont.)

Boulevard and Broad Street) that will take you down the bluff to Silver Beach Center and to the beach.

Lincoln Township Beach

5450 Notre Dame Avenue
Stevensville, MI 49127
269-429-1589

Lincoln Township Beach offers more than just sun and sand. When you first enter the park, there are several nature trails, lined with woodchips for easy walking. The trails feature informational signs about the various trees and plants you'll see during your walk. There's also a small picnic shelter, which holds three picnic tables. Follow the main road farther in to find more parking. There's a second picnic area overlooking some wetlands; come well-equipped with bug spray on still days. The beach area has a boardwalk and restrooms. There are some scenic trails that provide a nice lake view, and more covered picnic areas. The park will offer you a more private setting than Silver Beach on summer weekends.

Directions: From I-94, take exit 22, John Beers Rd, heading west. Make an almost immediate right onto Notre Dame Ave, which runs parallel to I-94. The entrance to Lincoln Township beach will be about 0.6 miles ahead on your left.

Lions Park Beach

1701 Lions Park Drive
St. Joseph, MI 49085
269-983-6341

Open daily 8 am - 10 pm

Silver Beach got the Parent's Magazine accolades, but Lions Park beach is also popular for families with young children. It's located just south of Silver Beach -- in fact, the two are within sight of each other. Take advantage of the free parking, or walk there along the Howard Family Trail, which is at one end at the beach. There is no admission charge, and Lions Park is usually much less crowded than Silver Beach. Kids enjoy a large selection of play equipment,

Lions Park Beach (cont.)

including a sprawling climbing structure, swings, and bouncers. The two-story twisty slide offers terrific views of the lighthouse and the lake. There are no concessions at Lions Park, but there are several covered picnic pavilions, and lots of small grills scattered around. Swinging benches are placed throughout the park and offer a welcome place to relax and enjoy the water. There is no lifeguard on duty, and truly, the swimming here is not very good. The beach drops into the water fairly steeply, and there are lots of rocks. Also, there are numerous short seawalls jutting into the water, and they create some choppy currents. In the winter, though, you can get an excellent view of the ice banks and dramatic waves without having to walk too far through the snow and sand. A small building offers restrooms in season. Trash cans are available for cleaning up after picnics.

Directions: From I-94, take exit 27, M-63/Niles Rd. Follow it into downtown St. Joseph. Turn left onto Park St, then left onto Lake Blvd. Return to Park St with an immediate right. Make a left onto Lions Beach Dr, which will dead-end at the parking lot for Lions Park Beach.

Madeline Bertrand County Park

3038 Adams Road
Niles, MI 49120
269-683-8280
www.berriencounty.org/parks

Open November - March: Wednesday - Sunday 10 am - 5 pm
April - October: Daily 10 am - sunset

Madeline Bertrand County Park is located south of Niles, on the border with Indiana. This is a popular park, and is well-staffed and maintained throughout the year. In the winter, there are several miles of cross-country skiing trails of varying difficulty. In the summer, the park offers mountain biking, hiking, and an 18-hole disc golf course. Best of all, rental equipment is available for a nominal fee, allowing families to try a new activity for minimal cost.

There is a charge of $3 per car to use the park; if you have purchased an annual permit for Berrien County Parks (including Silver Beach) you can use the permit here as well. Close to the parking lot is a play structure for young children. Picnic tables, grills, and shade trees make this a nice place for

Madeline Bertrand County Park (cont.)

informal get-togethers. Two of the three park shelters available for rental are also within a very short walk of the parking lot. The Topenebee Shelter is an open-air building with an enclosed area for serving food, while the Bertrand Lodge is fully enclosed. Both of these shelters take reservations up to two years in advance, as they are in high demand in the summer months. The third shelter overlooks the river and is a bit farther from the parking lot. All shelters include horseshoes and volleyball as part of their rental fee.

The Lodge holds the park management office. This is where you can pick up trail maps, and register to play the disc golf course. A day pass grants you unlimited games and costs $4 for adults and $3 for kids. Discs can be rented for an additional $1. Serious players will want to purchase their own discs, which are very different from the recreational Frisbees that you take to the beach. The discs used for golf are smaller, heavier, and made from stiffer plastic. The Lodge carries a wide selection, and they take credit cards. In the winter, the Lodge serves as a warming station for cross country skiiers, who enjoy the warmth from the fieldstone fireplace. Daily ski passes cost $4 per person, with ski rental costing an additional $10; the prices are lower for children. Next door to the Lodge is a final building where the restrooms are located; this building is open year-round.

There are three miles of trails in Madeline Bertrand Park. When conditions permit, these are groomed and reserved for cross-country skiiers. Check the website for updates on trail conditions before you leave. On Friday and Saturday nights, the trails are lit to allow nighttime skiing until 9 pm. If there isn't sufficient snow, the trails are open to hikers. In the summer, the longest trail welcomes mountain bikers in addition to hikers. All of the trails allow access to an observation deck over the St. Joseph River.

Directions: From US-31, take exit 3, Sturgis/New Buffalo. Turn left on Pulaski Highway/US-12, heading east. Travel 3.5 miles, then make a right on S. 3rd Street. Go another 2.2 miles, then turn right on Ontario Road. Ontario Road veers towards the left and becomes Adams Road. The entrance to Madeline Bertrand County Park will be on your right.

McCoy Pond Park

Buchanan, MI 49107

Open daily, dawn - dusk

If you are in the Buchanan area on a nice day and need to unwind for a moment, try tiny McCoy Pond Park. The gentle hills cradle a pond where a family of well-fed ducks live. There is a small footbridge over the pond, really a widening of a creek, and several benches facing the water. The creek enters from under Front Street and exits the park under a nearby industrial building, so the water does not stagnate. A small historical marker notes that the park was the site of a former ice rink and social center in the 1870's. It was later demolished for a factory expansion, an illustration of the importance of even small waterways in the early industrial era.

A single picnic table is present. There are no bathrooms or water fountains. You can purchase snacks, for yourselves and for the ducks, at a nearby gas station.

Directions: From US-31, take exit 4, Niles-Buchanan Rd, towards Buchanan. The park is on your right two miles down the Niles-Buchanan Road, where a small parking lot is available just before the intersection with Front Street.

Memorial Park

Berrien Springs, MI 49085

Open dawn - dusk daily

Memorial Park, located across from the History Center, is a nice place to drop by if your kids need a few minutes of physical activity. The park's main feature is a twenty foot stone pillar, which was erected in 1924, and is surrounded by tall fir trees. The engraved plaque commemorates veterans of the Civil War, the Spanish-American War, and the World War. There are some attractive flower beds surrounding the pillar. The side of the park farthest from busy Cass Street has a tall old-fashioned metal slide and some swings. There are a few picnic tables, some benches and trash cans. The park is not fenced, so adults will need to keep a close eye on toddlers.

Directions: From US-31, take exit 15, M-139 into the Village of Berrien Springs, where it becomes Cass Street. Memorial Park is located on the corner of Cass and Madison.

Milton Park

Corner of Niles and Winchester Avenues
St. Joseph, MI 49085

Open daily, dawn - dusk

Milton Park sits on the site of the former St. Joseph middle school. It's bordered on three sides by houses and on one side by Niles Avenue. A fence keeps kids from venturing out into the street. Milton Park is a quiet park in keeping with its residential setting, and a pleasant place to spend a few hours if you don't want to travel someplace crowded like Silver Beach.

Half of the park area is taken up by a circular blacktop path around a large grassy area. Beginning bike riders, as well as rollerbladers, will enjoy traveling around the path, which has just enough slopes to keep it interesting. There are benches for parents to sit and keep an eye on everything. The playground equipment is set in a sand pile. There is a climbing structure small enough for older toddlers, as well as swings and a merry-go-round. The cast concrete turtle and dolphin, set low to the ground and with rounded, abstract shapes, are particularly fun for younger children to explore.

There is an attractive chess table and benches made of gray polished stone. One of the park benches is made from cornerstones from the former schools that stood nearby. A drinking fountain runs during the warmer months. There are no bathrooms or picnic tables, but there is a small amphitheater with benches that serve as a nice place to sit. Supplies to clean up after dogs are provided, as are trash cans.

Directions: From I-94, take exit 27, M-63/Niles Rd, towards St. Joseph. Milton Park will be on your right as you approach the downtown area.

Napier Park

Intersection of Pontiac Road and Montezmua Road
Benton Harbor, MI 49022

Open dawn - dusk daily

Napier Park is a small residential park in the Fairplain neighborhood of Benton Harbor. It can be seen from busy Napier Avenue, but is set far back enough that the traffic is not a concern. Shaped like a triangle, it holds a selection of old

Napier Park (cont.)

fashioned playground equipment, including swings, slides and a jungle gym. There is a picnic bench and trashcan, but no bathrooms.

Directions: From I-94, take exit 28, M-139N/Scottdale Rd. Make a left onto Napier Ave. Turn right onto Pontiac Rd; Napier Park is located immediately ahead.

North Lake Park

Stevensville, MI 49127
Reserve pavilion by calling 269-429-1589 ext.10

Open daily, dawn - dusk

North Lake Park is on the bank of the one of the three Grand Mere lakes, which are separated from Lake Michigan by some large sand dunes. This park does not have access to Lake Michigan, but there is enough here to make it a pleasant place to spend an afternoon. The parking lot is right up against the grass, which slopes gently down to the lake. There is a modern play structure with particularly good climbing features and an unusually steep nine foot slide for daredevils. The ground is covered in soft woodchips for safety. There are swings for toddlers and older children as well. Large oaks provide shade, and there are grills and picnic benches scattered across the grounds. Take a walk out to the point for a near-360 view of the water, and enjoy it from the bench under a weeping willow. Use caution with smaller children, as there are no fences or barriers between the park and the water's edge.

Close to the water is the picnic pavilion; rental is $35 for residents of Lincoln Township and $50 for non-residents. The pavilion holds eight picnic tables and has pull-down walls if the weather is windy. There is a large grill adjacent to the pavilion. Bathrooms are located behind. There are trash cans provided throughout the park. Between the park and the pavilion, there are poles for a volleyball net. There is also a fire ring with benches, right next to the water. A dock allows boat launches onto North Lake. Duck blinds can be constructed with a permit.

Directions: From I-94, take exit 22 headed west on Grand Mere Road. Veer right onto Ice St. Parking for North Lake Park is on your right as Ice St ends.

Randall Park

Corner of Church and Tannery Streets
Coloma, MI 49038

Open 8 am - 10 pm daily
Supervised 4 pm - 10 pm

Randall Park is conveniently located just off I-94 in Coloma. Its fantastic play structure makes it well worth a stop. Kids from two to teen will enjoy clambering over the wooden fairy tale castle. For younger ones, the "Tot Lot" section is separately enclosed. Here, they can enjoy swings and small slides, a wooden teepee, a crawling tunnel, sand pit, balance beam and some musical instruments. Older children have the run of the towers, bridges, escape hatches, secret staircases and climbing ropes. The park is clean and well kept. The climbing area is bedded with mulch, and is fenced with only two entrances, so parents can make sure their children don't wander off.

Adjacent to the castle is a spacious shaded picnic pavilion, which holds eight tables comfortably. On the other side of the castle, a blacktop path traces a circle through pleasant lawns and a few small flowerbeds. Wheeled toys are not permitted in Randall Park, but people enjoy playing catch on the lawns or enjoying the sun and fresh air on some of the many benches. The park has a water fountain in the warmer months. There are no bathrooms, which seems a shame, since the park is such fun that kids may want to stay for several hours. There are thirty parking spaces on Tannery Drive, the ones farthest from Church Street are closest to the play structure entrance.

Driections: From I-94, take exit 39; head north on Church St into Coloma. Make a right on Tannery St into the parking lot for Randall Park.

Riverfront Park

W Main and Front Streets
Niles, MI 49120

Open daily 8 am - 10 pm

Riverfront Park is the crown jewel of Niles' extensive park system. It is long and narrow, and encompasses two-thirds of the east bank of the Saint Joseph River within the City. Riverfront Park offers a fabulous array of recreational

Riverfront Park (cont.)

options for a variety of ages. Those with children ranging from 5 to 12 will find a large playground structure in a shaded area near the river and ample parking. Picnic tables and benches are adjacent to the structure. For those parents who also have children that are just a bit older, a 16,000 square foot skate park was developed in 2004 at the north end of the park. It is one of the finest publicly owned skate parks in Michigan, boasting large bowls as well as a street course. Parking for the skate park is available on the west side of Front Street. North of the skate park are two beach volleyball courts.

Just south of the playground structure is a pavilion (known locally as the Riverfront Amphitheater) which hosts three free musical performances every week from the beginning of June to the middle of August. The Niles Summer Concert Series offers live acts on Wednesdays, Thursday and Sunday evenings. The schedule may be found at www.nilesmainstreet.org. Music is easily heard from the playground.

Although there are a handful of Porta-Johns to serve the public, park users also have access to spacious and convenient restrooms in the Wonderland Cinema, which is located adjacent to Riverfront Park. The rear entrance of the Wonderland is a short walk from the playground, and across the street from municipal parking. Not many people are aware, but the owners of the Wonderland grant park users access to the movie theater's restrooms.

Directions: From US-31, take exit 5, Niles-Buchanan Rd, towards Niles. The road becomes Grant St as you enter the city. Make a left onto Lincoln Ave, then a right onto W Main St. Cross over the River and make the first left onto Front St. There are municipal parking lots with excellent access to Riverfront Park on your immediate left.

Riverview Park

2927 Niles Rd.
St. Joseph, MI 49085
269-983-6325

Open year-round
6 AM - 10 PM daily

If you're invited to a party in Riverview Park, make sure to get directions. Otherwise, you could get lost in the 107 acres. The entrance is off Niles Avenue,

Riverview Park (cont.)

between Nye's Apple Barn and Riverview Cemetary. As you travel down a hill towards the river, you'll see nature trails and the first of two large picnic pavilions, which can be rented through St. Joseph's recreation department. Continue driving into the park and pass the Tiscornia Boys Field, dedicated in 1955 in honor of a former mayor of St. Joseph. This is a full-fledged baseball field with bleachers and dugouts. Nearby, there is a small playground with swings, slides and a few picnic tables. Farther along the road is the second pavilion, which has an indoor space including a wood-burning fireplace, as well as bathrooms. Outside picnic tables and freestanding grills are available for parties when the weather is nice. The Woodbine pavillion has the best playground in the park. The structures all look like dinosaurs - climb up the backbone of a stegosaurus or swing off the outstretched wings of a pterodactyl. The play surface consists of six inches of shredded tires and is remarkably bouncy to walk on. In addition to the Boys Field, there are other soccer and baseball playing fields. A boat launch offers access to the St. Joseph River. You can stroll along the banks of the river; the park is a popular fishing spot.

Bathrooms are available during the warmer months at several widely spaced points throughout the park. There are bags to collect dog waste and plenty of trash receptacles. Unleashed animals are not permitted in Riverview Park. There is no fee for entry.

Directions: From I-94, take exit 27, M-63/Niles Ave, towards St. Joseph. The entrance to Riverview Park will be just ahead on your right and is well marked with a blue sign.

Rocky Gap Park

Benton Harbor, MI 49022

Open April - October, dawn - dusk

Tucked into a quiet residential neighborhood, just a mile or so from downtown St Joseph, is Rocky Gap Beach. The overlook platform situated high on a bluff provides beautiful views of the Lake Michigan shoreline. Climb down the dune to the pristine beach below, where the real fun begins. Glistening along the surf of this small beach are perfectly polished bits of beach glass. An artful hand can turn these colorful bits into jewelry and other crafts. Along with hunting for beach glass, this secluded and serene respite is a favorite lunchtime spot for nearby workers. It is also the perfect place to sunbathe with a good

Rocky Gap Park (cont.)

book, take a sunset stroll, or just sit and listen to the waves. Even on a hot summer weekend, the beach is sparsely populated, and sunbathers can spread far enough apart to give each other privacy. Rocky Gap is dog-friendly and is also designated as a kite-surfing beach. There is ample free parking and it is easy to find. The tradeoff for all the privacy is a lack of amenities; there are no restrooms, lifeguards or drinking fountains.

From I-94, take exit 27, M-63/Niles Ave, and follow it to the intersection with Main St. Make a right on Main St and cross over the St. Joseph River. Turn left onto Golf Rd, then make a sharp left onto Rocky Gap Rd. Rocky Gap Park will be on your right.

Roosevelt Elementary School

2000 El Dorado Dr.
Stevensville, MI 49127
www.lakeshoreschools.k12.mi.us/roosevelt/index.htm

Available when school is not in session.

On nice days when school is not in session, pack up the bikes and head to Roosevelt Elementary's playground. Their "safety circle" feature is a terrific place for a ride. Spread out over the area of a soccer field, you'll find paved trails with lane markings, real road signs, marked crosswalks, and even a working traffic light! Kids love to bike on what appears to be a real street. When they're finished with the bikes, they'll enjoy the large playground, set on wood chips, that has some of the best climbing available in the county. We especially love the obstacle course for playing "follow the leader." There's also two tetherball poles, basketball hoops and soccer fields. The whole area is enormous and doesn't offer much shade or wind protection; on the other hand, it's a great place to fly kites. As is appropriate for an elementary school, this playground is suitable for kids five and up.

There's a chain link fence around the safety circle, with entries at the parking lot as well as to a trail leading to the Lincoln Township library. Dogs on leashes are welcome along the walk - make sure to enjoy the humorous sign for dogs and their owners at the parking lot. Of course, the playground is off limits to visitors during school hours. The traffic light is not always turned on; we wish it were.

Roosevelt Elementary School (cont.)

Directions: From I-94, take exit 23, onto Marquette Woods heading east. Make a right onto Cleveland Ave. Turn right on El Dorado Dr; there will be a small sign for Roosevelt Elementary. El Dorado Dr ends at the parking lot for the school, adjacent to the playground.

Silver Beach County Park

101 Broad Street
St. Joseph, Michigan 49085
269-982-0533

Open daily 5 am - sunset
Parking charges from April - October

Named one of the top 10 family beaches in the country by Parents Magazine, Silver Beach is a wonderful family destination.

There's something here to please almost everyone. Kids enjoy the play structures, and on days with calm water, the water stays shallow for a great distance. Swimming and body surfing are popular, and in the spring and fall, you can watch kite-boarders and surfers in full bodysuits take on more challenging waves. Silver Beach boasts the sugar sands that have made this stretch of Lake Michigan famous, and volleyball players pick up more than their fair share on the extensive courts. This is also the place for summer sunbathing, and on beautiful days the huge beach can get quite crowded with towels and umbrellas.

You also can rent kayaks from a nearby vendor, go fishing along the pier and walk the half-mile (barrier free) walkway that runs along the St. Joseph River. The park hosts outdoor concerts during the summer. This is one of the few county parks that is staffed by lifeguards in the summer months. The concession stand offers burgers and cold drinks, as well as restrooms. There are a number of picnic pavilions. Many people order a to-go pizza from nearby Silver Beach Pizza to serve as their picnic.

Residents and long-term visitors should make sure to purchase an annual park pass, which grants entry to Silver Beach as well as several other county parks. Otherwise, there is a $6 charge for Berrien County residents, and an $8 charge for non-residents (charged on a per-car basis.)

Tiscornia Beach

80 Ridgeway Dr.
St. Joseph MI 49085

Open daily 6 am - 10 pm
Parking charge on summer weekends

Just north of Silver Beach is Tiscornia Beach, where you can enjoy all that summer has to offer, but without the crowds. Located on the quieter side of the channel, this park is a beach-goer's paradise. With beautiful white sand beaches and lots of shoreline access for swimming and splashing, this is the perfect spot to while away a summer day. Pack a lunch to enjoy in the picnic area with plenty of tables, grills, and trashcans. There is also a covered pavilion with more tables for a bit of shade or shelter from passing sprinkles. On summer weekends, non-residents pay a fee to park in the lot, which is also the parking lot for the North Pier Lighthouse. Although a bit tricky to find at first, once you find Tiscornia Beach, you'll want to keep coming back. There are restrooms available, and dogs are welcome but must remain leashed.

Directions: From I-94, take exit 27, M-63/Niles Ave, into town. Veer right onto Main St and cross the river. After crossing the river, take the first left onto Momany Dr. Turn left on Upton St and follow this to Marina Dr. You will pass the marina and the St. Joseph River Yacht Club. Then turn right on Ridgeway Dr. Tiscornia Beach will be on your right.

Tiny Tots Park

Corner of Willa Street and Botham Avenue
St. Joseph, MI 49085

Open daily, dawn - dusk

If you have some smaller kids that need to burn off energy, take them to Tiny Tots. This is a pleasant small city park located behind First Church of God on Niles Avenue in Saint Joseph. It occupies a corner lot, and there's plenty of street parking available. The park is fenced, so you don't need to worry about kids running into the streets, which are pretty quiet anyway. There are a few picnic tables and benches.

The big attraction at Tiny Tots is the climbing structure shaped like a pirate

TinyTots (cont.)

ship. Little ones can let their imagination soar as they turn the ship's wheel and enjoy two climbing levels. The surrounding ground is covered in a thick layer of shredded tires, which makes for a soft landing as they negotiate the slides and ladders. While the ship is the biggest piece of equipment, there are also climbing bars and swings, including those with bucket seats for toddlers. A small merry-go-round completes the suite of classic playground favorites. There is ample grassy space for running around.

The shredded tires that cover the ground can sneak into open shoes and mark white clothes, so have kids wear sneakers and playclothes that can get dirty.

There are no bathrooms nearby. A water fountain runs during the warmer months. The area around the ship holds rainwater and snowmelt, so save Tiny Tots for drier days.

Directions: From I-94, take exit 27, M-63/Niles Ave, heading north. Take a right onto Botham Ave. Tiny Tots will be on your left.

Weko Beach

Bridgman, MI 49106
www.bridgman.org/weko

Daily beach pass fee and other camping fees apply

With 900 feet of spectacular Lake Michigan Beach, Weko Beach and Campground is the ideal family destination. The wide and spacious beach is perfect for a long walk or jog as well as hours of fun playing in the sand and water. Tucked on the other side of the dune is the campground. Campers can enjoy one of the twenty-two primitive sites or reserve one of the four log cabins. Amenities include hot showers, clean bathrooms, a dump station, and outdoor grills. Pets are welcome in the campground only and must be leashed. From the campground, explorers can enjoy a winding hiking trail through the woods. Connecting the beach and campground is a boardwalk that crosses over a small stream and climbs up to several overlooks with sweeping views of the coast. Grab lunch or a snack at the lovely beach house café. Or pack your own picnic to enjoy at the many picnic tables and outdoor grills. In the evenings a bugler plays Taps as the sun goes down. It's an awesome thing to hear especially for those who have been in the military.

Weko Beach (cont.)

When the kids need a break from tumbling in the waves, walk over to the playground or take a nice stroll into downtown Bridgman to enjoy the local farmers' market or Sherman's ice cream. Coupled with a tour of nearby vineyards or a trip to Warren Dunes, Weko Beach is a great place to bring your family for the day or weekend.

Directions: From I-94, take exit 16, Red Arrow Highway. Travel north one mile, then make a left at the first light, Lake St. Lake St dead-ends into Weko Beach.

INTRODUCTION

Nurturing a child's desire to run and play is important to all of us. In a Montessori context, sports activities involve striving for one's personal best. It's not that there is never competition, but the emphasis is on working as a team to achieve excellence. Southwest Michigan offers many opportunities to practice these skills and get exercise in family-friendly environments. Whether your passion is canoeing, fishing, sailing, ice skating, or tobogganing, you can find what you need in the pages that follow.

Charter Fishing

www.swmichigan.org/entertainment/fishing.html

Year-round

There are a lot of charter fishing companies in Berrien County. They offer charters on Lake Michigan, inland lakes and rivers. There are essentially two main fishing experiences available: private charters, where you fish for salmon and other sport fish, and perch boats, where large groups of up to forty people fish. The descriptions below are generalizations; confirm any details with the charter company of your choice.

Private charters are usually booked for either half-day or full-day excursions. Start times are early (leaving the dock at 6 am) to take advantage when the fish are biting best. A half day ends around 11 am; a full day ends at 3 pm. Generally, you pay for a half-day (6 am - 11 am) or whole day (6 am - 3 pm). A flat fee covers usually four people; additional people incur an extra charge. The boats have covered cabins so if it's raining, you can fish under cover. On charters, the crew manages all the gear, casts the lines, and notifies you when a fish is on the line. You reel, and the crew nets the fish. The fish are kept in the cooler and cleaned by the crew on the dock. You need a fishing license; if this is your only outing for the year, the cheapest option is to buy a one-day license from the charter company. Salmon fishing can take place either on Lake Michigan or on the local rivers. Charters generally do not cancel except for violent thunderstorms.

Perch fishing takes place on a big boat with up to 40 people, so you will be fishing next to people you don't know. Captain Hook Charters is the only company that offers the big perch boat. There is plenty of indoor cabin space.

Charter Fishing (cont.)

They anchor the boat and everyone fishes off the sides and back. You can bring you own poles, or rent a pole for a nominal additional fee. You will bait your own hook and decide when to haul in your fish. There are buckets provided to hold your catch. Limit for perch fishing is set by state law and is 35 fish per person. A fishing license is required; again, if you don't have one, you can buy a one-day license from the company. The crew will clean your catch on the docks for an extra fee; they are fast at this, but it may add some additional time to your trip. The perch boat is very kid-friendly and probably the best introduction to fishing. The railing on the perch boat is chest-high, which makes sitting difficult. Consider bringing a book or other distraction for your child in case of boredom. A trip usually lasts three hours. Perch fishing always takes place on Lake Michigan.

Bring a cooler packed with lunch and beverages for your party; it is customary to bring food to offer the crew on a charter trip. The perch boats have a wet bar, and BYOB is not allowed. Dress in layers, as it is often cooler on the water than it is on land. Bring sunscreen and seasickness remedies. If there's no wind, flies can bite, so bug repellent comes in handy.

Clear Lake Equestrian Center

1207 E Galien/ Buchanan Road
Buchanan MI 49107
269-591-1833
on Facebook: search Clear Lake Equestrian Center

Located in Buchanan, Clear Lake Equestrian Center offers something for novices who have never been around horses, all the way to experienced riders who want to compete in equestrian sports. Melissa Ashcraft is an experienced horsewoman who travelled with the world-famous Lipizzaner stallions for five years. She is friendly and approachable, and will work with you to select the best experience for your family.

For those just looking for an introduction to horse riding, check out the camps, which run spring through fall. Kids are divided by experience, starting with "Pre-pony" camp, geared towards ages 5 - 7. Pre-pony lasts a single half-day; kids are able to interact with and groom the horses on the ground, then take a ride if they are comfortable doing so. Kids ages 8 and up start with Beginner camp, then work their way through Intermediate and Advanced. All of these

Clear Lake Equestrian Center (cont.)

camps are available in either weekend or week-long day camps, with a day running from 9 am - 5 pm. Campers bring their own lunches; on Friday, at the end of the week-long camp, there's a pizza lunch, followed by a mini-show for parents and family to attend. Camps are open to a maximum of ten to twelve riders, and there is a 1:2 staff member ratio. There is a strong emphasis on safety. Riders must wear long pants and low-heeled boots; helmets are strongly encouraged. Kids can wear bike helmets if they don't want to invest in a riding helmet right away. Pre-pony camp costs $40/child; the cost for the more advanced camps averages $80 per child per day. Sign up at least one week in advance; there may be a discount offered for early registration. Parents are encouraged to stay during the pre-pony sessions; younger siblings are welcome to enjoy the fresh air and watch the mini-horses that live at the center.

Clear Lake also offers private lessons for $45/hr; add more riders to the lesson for reduced rates. Students can receive instruction in dressage, English, jumping, Western, natural horsemanship and showmanship. Competition is not required, but there is a show team for those that want to participate. The center hosts birthday parties, available for all ages and a wide number of kids. At parties, kids can ride and pet the horses, and rent a mini-horse and cart. Barn staff will lead all the horses for safety. For those that own their own horse, full boarding with 12' by 12' boxstall and large grass pastures costs $325/month.

Directions: From US-31, take exit 3, US-12, towards Sturgis/New Buffalo. Travel 3.7 miles, then turn right onto Bakertown Rd. Take the second left onto E. Galien Buchanan Rd. Clear Lake Equestrian Center will be on your right.

Doe-Wah-Jack's Canoe Rental

52963 M 51 N
Dowagiac, MI 49047
269-782-7410
www.paddledcri.com

June - August: Open daily 10 am - 6 pm
May, October, and November: Weekends only

Beginning canoers and kayakers will enjoy the gentle Dowagiac River, and Doe-Wah-Jack's Canoe Rental offers a perfect introduction. The unusual business name gives you the proper local pronunciation of Dowagiac; the emphasis is on the second syllable. Doe-Wah-Jack's rents canoes, as well as single and

Doe-Wah-Jack's Canoe Rental (cont.)

double kayaks, and there are three different trip lengths to choose from. You keep count of the bridges you cross under to find your take-out spots. Trips are meant to take two, four or six hours. If you are travelling in a single car, you first follow the staff to the designated take-out spot, leave your car, and return in the staff car to start your trip. There is an extra $12 charge for this service.

The Dowagiac River averages two to four feet deep. The top half of the river is about 40-60 feet wide, while the bottom half ranges from 50 to 100 feet wide. Much of the time, the river has a canopy of trees, which provides a measure of shade and lends a quiet, green atmosphere. The river is 90% spring-fed, and the water is cool and clear. This plus the shade keeps the temperature cool even on very hot days. Doe-Wah-Jack staff groom the river and try to keep it portage-free. In all, this is an excellent place to introduce children to the joys of canoeing.

The canoes are aluminum; a seat cushion is provided for each person as part of the rental. There is a maximum of three people per canoe. For a family of four, we suggest renting two two-person kayaks. These offer spacious seating and sit relatively low in the water, providing an extra measure of stability for novice boaters. Kid-sized paddles are available and allow everyone to participate.

On the banks of the river, you will see perhaps a total of six houses during your trip. The longer routes take you through virgin forest. Start early in the day and stay quiet to improve your chances of seeing wildlife. The owner, Randy Rea, is very knowledgeable about the geology and history of the area and is a great resource if you have questions about what you'll see on your trip.

Doe-Wah-Jack's gets busy during the summer months. Reservations are always recommended; the form is available for downloading on their website. There is a $10 deposit required for each vessel. A two-hour trip for two people costs $42; rates for longer trips are available on the website. Please note that they do not take credit cards.

Directions: From I-94, take exit 30, E Napier Ave/US-31 S. Continue onto MI-152 E. After ten miles, MI-152 makes a right; continue to follow it as it again bends left through the Sister Lakes. Make a right onto M 51 N/MI-51 S. Doe-Wah-Jack's will be on your left.

Five Pines

6597 Smith Road
Berrien Center, MI 49102
269-471-1396
www.fivepines.org

Saturdays 11 am - 5 pm
Sundays 1 pm - 5:30 pm

Five Pines has several seasonal activities open to the general public. In the fall, groups can enjoy a hayride, while in winter, cross country skiing and snow tubing are popular.

The hayrides take some planning. You must call ahead to reserve a date and time; they start taking reservations months in advance. There are no individual tickets; instead, you rent the entire wagon, which can seat up to twenty. Included in the $75 fee is a thirty minute hayride, followed by an hour around the fire pit. Five Pines includes everything you need for a fun campfire, iuncluding wood and the sticks to roast your marshmallows and hot dogs.

Winter sports at Five Pines can fit more easily into a spontaneous weekend outing. Check the website in advance to see if there's enough snow. They do have a snowmaking machine to keep the ski trails and tubing runs open in case of a mild thaw. A day pass for tubing costs $8 for adults and $7 for kids age 6 - 11; 5 and under ride free. Cross country skiing passes are $7 for adults and $5 for kids; a flat fee of $3 applies if you bring your own equpiment. The skiing trail is a mile long with both flat and hilly regions, so skiiers of all abilities can find terrain that suits them. The tubing hill has three lanes for tubers, separated by low walls of snow. Adults can ride with a small child on the same tube. You do need to carry your tube back up the hill each time, which can be a difficult task for younger kids. Staff members will be happy to demonstrate different games that make the tubing even more fun.

Frequent visitors should check out the season passes for great deals on skiing and tubing. If you have a large group, there are special rates available. The website often has coupons for concessions at the warming shelter, where you can buy pizza, hot dogs, and cocoa.

Directions: From US-31, take exit 15, MI-139S/ Old US 31S, towards Berrien Springs. Turn left on W. Ferry St. and cross the river. Make a left on Dean's Hill Rd. and an immediate right on Pokagon Rd. Turn left on Smith Rd. Five Pines Ministries will be on your left; there is a large sign.

St Joseph / Lakeshore Football game

St. Joseph Bears
Dickinson Stadium
www.stjoefootball.com

Lakeshore Lancers
Al Stockman Stadium
www.lakeshorefb.com

The St. Joseph - Lakeshore Football Game is a long and storied rivalry. After a long period of Lakeshore Lancer dominance, the Bears have enjoyed a resurgence in recent years, and the game is now closely contested. The teams play each other once a year, alternating home field advantage. While any of the games are fun, the Bears-Lancers rivalry makes that game a special event that involves most of the surrounding community. General admission tickets at either stadium are only $5 per person.

St. Joseph:
Tickets for the rivalry game go on sale several days in advance, and can be purchased at either high school during the school day. The gates open ninety minutes before kickoff. There is lots of parking available close to the high school, including student lots as well as the large lot between Roxy's and Kelley's Bowl, but this is an extremely well-attended game, and spaces can fill up quickly. The side lot north of the practice field is open to tailgating. Alcohol and tobacco are not appropriate on school property, and there is no place to dispose of charcoal.

Inside, you can purchase game programs at the ticket booth or the concession stands. They also sell snack food to raise money for the football team and the band. There are two stands under the home seating area (one of which also sells team apparel), and a third stand in the northwest corner of the stadium. We love that there are changing tables in all the restrooms. You can bring seat-back chairs to make the bleachers more comfortable.

Lakeshore:
The season schedule is mailed out to households in the school district, but can also be found on the school website. To purchase tickets, stop by the school office a week in advance of the game, or take your chance at the gate. Don't expect to use the main school parking lot. Try the side lot facing John Beers Road; the shopping areas across the street allow overflow parking as well. Plan to walk some distance to get to the game. Games usually start at 7:30; show up an hour or more in advance to get a seat. Reserve sections are available for boosters and season ticket holders. Seats near the band are popular for families. Tailgating is popular in the school parking lot, and tailgaters often start

High School Football Games (cont.)

at 4 or 5 pm. Bring grills, flags, food, chairs, footballs. This is a very family-friendly scene. Within the school building, you can buy pop and hot dogs.

The football stadium is beautiful, with new turf. Each time the home team scores, fireworks are set off beyond the end zone - this can be loud for small children, so warn them to plug their ears. The Lakeshore marching band is excellent; make sure to catch the pregame show. Concessions are available throughout the game - popcorn, hot pretzels, hot dogs, nachos, candy, coffee, hot chocolate and pop. The stands are manned by band boosters to raise money for the band.

John and Dede Howard Ice Rink

2414 Willa Drive
St. Joseph, MI 49085
269-983-8795
www.sjcity.com

Saturdays 11 am - 5 pm
Sundays 1 pm - 5:30 pm

Michigan certainly gets plenty of winter weather. Make the best of it at the public Howard Ice Arena. The season runs late November or early December until mid-March. It is an outdoor ice rink with a roof, so come prepared based on the current weather conditions. Check the web site for the open skate schedule, as it can vary over school break. Enjoy some brisk outdoor exercise, or watch the skaters from the low bleacher seats lining one side of the rink. You can warm up by the wood burning stove in the warming building while you take a break or change into or out of your skates. The Center Ice Snack Bar and restrooms are located within. The snack bar sells candy, chips, pop, and a few hot items such as nachos and hot dogs.

Daily admission is $5 per person, with an additional $3 for skate rental. Frequent skaters can purchase a season pass to save money. In the warmer months, the arena can be rented for in-line skating. During the winter, the facility can be rented for private events. Plan this well in advance, as a very popular local hockey league plays here.

Directions: From I-94, take exit 27, Niles Rd, towards St. Joseph. Make a right onto Napier Ave; the rink will be on your left almost immediately. Take the next left onto Willa Dr to enter the parking lot.

Power in Motion Gym

3889 S. M-139
St. Joseph, MI 49085
269-429-5100

Hours and class schedules vary.

Power in Motion is a well-run gymnastics facility. The staff is very enthusiastic and dedicated to safety. With a new building built in November 2009, and lots of new equipment, it also makes for good clean fun. Gymnastics classes for boys and girls of all ages are available. On any given night, you will find the youngest of gymnasts and tumblers stretching, running obstacle courses, and practicing balancing and muscle strengthening games. You will also see older kids practicing vault, beam, rings, uneven/paralell bars, and floor routines. The highlight for everyone is the trampoline runway (Tumble Trak) that leads to a huge foam pit.

On cold winter Saturdays, they have open gym time where everyone can shake their wiggles out. Admission is $5 per person. The gym is also an outstanding place to have a birthday party. The high-energy staff of at least three runs the entire party. Included are active games and a pinata, and the staff also facilitate the gift opening. The kids definitely sleep well after a birthday party at Power in Motion.

Directions: From I-94, take exit 28, M-139, heading south. Power in Motion will be on your right, set a little back from the road. The front of the building is well-marked with a sign.

Redbud Track and Trail

13638 N. Redbud Trail
Buchanan, MI 49107
269-695-6405
www.redbudmx.com

Various weekends, April - October 9 AM - 6 PM
Check website for race weekends

Motocross, short for motorcycle cross country, originated in France and was popularized in this country in the ESPN X games. You can see both amateur and professional motocross at Rebdud Track and Trail. Races are held during

Redbud Track and Trail (cont.)

the summer approximately every third weekend. Tickets can be purchased at the gate ($10 for adults, kids under 12 are free); practice gets underway about 9 AM. There is seating in bleachers as well as grassy areas; feel free to bring chairs and blankets. Enjoy a picnic while you watch racers, who can range in age from four to over sixty, speed across the hilly dirt track. Grilled concessions are available, and coolers are welcomed, but glass containers are not permitted. The seating area is about a five minute walk from the parking lot. Pets are welcome as long as they are on a leash. The bikes are loudest at the starting gate, so seating at other parts of the track may be more suitable for smaller children.

The amateur races tend to be family events, as children of all ages participate in the races. On the Fourth of July weekend, Redbud hosts a professional motocross meet. Tickets are still available for gate purchase, but are more expensive - $35 for adults and $10 for kids. During the pro events, there are areas set aside for family groups who want to enjoy the races but avoid the louder parties. There are special kids' activities such as a climbing wall and bounce castle, which charge a small additional fee. Vendors offer T-shirts and souvenirs for sale. You can leave the park and return later in the day on the same ticket.

The bathroom facilities are limited to portapotties during amateur events. Water and pop can be purchased at the concession stand.

Directions: US-31 south to Exit 13; make a right off the ramp. Make a right on to Redbud Trail at the stop sign. Redbud Track and Trail is easily visible three miles down the road, on the right.

Sport Fit Athletics

2560 South Cleveland Avenue
St Joseph, MI 49085
269-983-3169
www.sportfitathletics.com

Open gym: noon - 2 pm on Saturdays
Class times vary; call for schedule

Sport Fit Athletics (formerly Cheer Unlimited) gives kids the opportunity to learn gymnastics. Its classes start at the toddler level and continue on through

Sport Fit Athletics (cont.)

competitive cheer. Did you ever wonder how gymnasts first try out the uneven bars? Stop by the gym and you'll learn their secret - the bars are set in a giant pit filled with soft foam blocks and a trampoline bottom. During open gym, you have the chance to run around on the bouncy floor and Tumble Trak, which is essentially a long trampoline set flush with the floor. Kids have lots of fun leaping into the foam pit, then clambering back out. The foam blocks do tend to shed bits of blue fuzz, so wear old clothes and plan to change at the end. Also, there are no shoes permitted in the tumbling area, so wear socks. Small balls are lots of fun as the kids bounce around, and can be in short supply - consider bringing your own. Open gym is a fun time to check out the equipment and costs $7 per person.

Sport Fit Athletics takes children as young as 18 months old. Classes are designed by age and skill level. They are offered in ten week sessions throughout the year. Classes for kids ages 6 and up are often divided by gender. There are a range of classes to suit different levels of interest. Sibling discounts are available Also, the gym is a fun place for children's birthday parties. The new owners of the gym are introducing new features all the time, so check their website or call them if you have a particular need.

Directions: From I-94, take exit 27, Niles Rd., heading north towards St. Joseph. Make a left on Hilltop Rd., then take the second left onto Cleveland Ave. Sport Fit Athletics will be on your right; it is located in a multi-unit commerical building.

St. Joseph Junior Foundation

Lighthouse Lane
St. Joseph, MI 49085
269-983-5441
www.sjjf.org

St. Joseph Junior Foundation located on Lighthouse Lane, just east of the St. Joseph River Yacht Club, offers youth sailing, youth racing and adult sailing classes starting in mid-June and going through August. The youth classes accomodate children from ages 8-17. They must be able to swim the length of the clubhouse pool and tread water.

The program is based on the US Sailing training system. Students always wear life jackets. Instructors are either in the student's boat or on a safety boat in the student's immediate vicinity. The instructors are energetic young adults,

St. Joseph Junior Foundation (cont.)

many of whom have learned to sail through this program. The classes are structured so that they are able to accomodate students with varying levels of experience including students who have never experienced boating of any kind. While water safety is stressed, the instructors use a variety of water games to teach all of the important elements of sailing on Lake Michigan including rigging, navigation, and recovering from a capsize.

Directions: From I-94, take exit 27, Niles Ave, heading north. Veer right onto Main St and cross the St Joseph River. Take the Momany Drive exit on your left; turn left onto Edgewater Drive at the bottom of the hill. Take the cobblestone street until it ends at Marina Drive. Take a sharp left onto Marina Dr. Follow Marina Dr around West Basin Marina. Make a left onto Ridgeway, and another left onto Lighthouse Ln.

Three Oaks Spokes Bicycle Club

3 Central
Three Oaks, MI 49128
269-756-3361
www.applecidercentury.com/spokes.htm

Bicycle rides are a terrific family activity If you're not sure where to ride or how to get started, consider visiting the Three Oaks Spokes Bicycle Club at their location in the Dewey Cannon Trading Company in Three Oaks, behind the Vickers Theater. Here you can obtain tourist and cycling information, rent bicycles for you and bike trailers for the kids to ride in, and pick up some healthy snacks for the ride. Three Oaks Spokes has designated twelve self-guided tours on paved back roads around the Three Oaks area. The routes for the tours range in length from 5 to 60 miles, and follow secondary roads over rushing streams and through picturesque rolling hills, patchwork farmland and beautiful meadows, parks and forests. While visiting Three Oaks, stop by the Three Oaks Township Public Library to view a collection of historic bicycles owned by Three Oaks Spokes, including one bike dating from the 1860's.

Directions: From I-94, take exit 12 toward Sawyer. Turn left at Sawyer Rd, then take the 3rd left onto 3 Oaks Rd and go 5 miles. Continue onto N. Elm St, turn right at Central Ave, and take the 3rd right onto Central. The club will be on your left.

NOTES:

INTRODUCTION

In Montessori philosophy there is a concept called supranature that refers to the relationship between humanity and nature. Since the study of history is essentially the study of human beings on earth, this relationship is an integral part of human history. In studying the Timeline of Humanity, Brookview students gain an understanding of the symbiotic relationship between our planet and its inhabitants and develop a deep respect for the environment. Further exposure to the majesty of nature through camping and hiking not only heightens this respect, but is also tons of fun. Enjoyment of the great outdoors in this beautiful region is always time well spent.

Bear Cave Resort

4085 Bear Cave Road
Buchanan, MI 49107
269-695-3050

May 1 - September 30
Cave hours: 9 am - 12 noon and 1:30 p.m. - 4:30 p.m. daily

Anyone with an interest in geology should be sure to visit the only cave in the Great Lakes area, just ten minutes from downtown Buchanan. Bear Cave Resort, previously open to members only, is now open to the public. Located overlooking the St. Joseph River, the resort has camping hookups for RVs, as well as tent sites with fire rings. An archway at the end of the parking lot leads you down to the office, which holds both the gift shop and the entrance to the cave. The walk through the forest is paved, but the hill is a bit steep. The cave itself has stairs, and there is a place to park strollers at the office.

Bear Cave is formed from tufa limestone, which distinguishes it from most of the caverns in the United States. Within the cave is a large boulder deposited by a glacier several thousand years ago. There is a wide variety of rock formations, including stalactites and stalagmites, travertine and tufa rocks, and fossil imprints. Cave pearls, which form when calcite precipitates around a nucleus within running water, have also been found in Bear Cave. The cave opens onto a waterfall, but that exit has been blocked to prevent vandalization. The waterfall can be seen from outside the cave, and the resort provides a trail there with a bridge to better see into the cavern. The cave tour takes about ten minutes and is self-guided, with audio commentary from speakers placed

Bear Cave Resort (cont.)

along the path. The fee is $2 per adult, $1 for kids age 7-12, kids six and under are free. There are numerous small bats in the cave that will fly around if they are disturbed. The famous silent movie "The Great Train Robbery" was filmed in part here, and the cave is rumored to have been a stop on the Underground Railroad.

If not camping, you can purchase a day pass to take advantage of everything the resort offers. A pass for a group of four costs $10; additional people are $2/ each. There is an arcade room, pool table, shuffleboard and volleyball courts, and a pool with a hot tub. Bathroom and laundry facilities are available. Picnics are welcome. Packaged snacks are available at the gift shop.

Directions: From US-31, take exit 13, Snow Rd, traveling west. Take the first left onto Red Bud Trail. Bear Cave Road will be on your left; there is a large sign.

Butler Tree Farm and Campground

21515 Crane Street
Dowagiac, MI 49047
269-782-4650
www.butlertrees.com

Pumpkins: late September - Halloween
Saturday and Sunday 10 am - 6 pm
Thursday and Friday 2 pm - 6 pm

Christmas trees: November 27 - December 23
Saturday and Sunday 10 am - 5:30 pm
Monday - Friday 1 pm - 5:30 pm

Camping: May - December

It's an hour's drive from St. Joseph, but well worth it. Sam and Brenda Butler believe every family deserves the chance to select their own, live Christmas tree. Butler Tree farm grows eight types of evergreen trees, including Balsam, Douglas, Fraser Fir, Scotch Pine, White Pine, Blue Spruce, White Spruce, and Concolor. The trees have been shaped as they grow to provide that perfect Christmas tree silhouette. You can cut your own as Butler provides the saws and tree carts or have someone cut a tree for you. They provide the typical

Butler Tree Farm and Campground (cont.)

tree service of shaking, netting, and drilling holes into the bottom of the tree as well as selling tree stands. On weekends during the fall and winter, enjoy wagon rides and a small petting zoo. During the fall season, you can wander the pumpkin patch to find the perfect gourd. During the Christmas season, kids can visit with Santa.

This is a great tree farm even when it is cold since the trees are close to the parking lot and the wagon rides can be short or long depending on the weather. Blankets are provided on the wagon ride to keep the seats warm or to wrap yourself in. The wagon rides are a big hit with the kids, as holiday music is played and there is a lot to look at on the property.

The craft shop offers a large variety of gifts including hand crafted collectibles, wood carvings, lawn furniture and ornaments, custom built log furniture and more. It is a perfect spot to warm up next to the wood burning stove and have a warm cup of cocoa or apple cider. You also have the opportunity to pick up some baked goods at the Goodie shop that offers pies, breads, cakes and muffins.

If you want to get away for the weekend and not go far, this is the place to go to relax or explore with your family. For those that don't have tents, the log cabins are a great choice; bedding and lanterns are provided. Camping is available from May through December and all campsites and cabins include a picnic table and chairs, campfire pit and complimentary firewood. Some campsites include a covered pavilion with a picnic table and chairs to protect you from outdoor elements. Pets and horses are welcome.

Directions: From I-94, take exit 56, MI-51 S, towards Decatur/Dowagiac. Make a left on S George St. in Decatur, then the third right onto E Bronson St. Make a left on Co Rd 668, which becomes Decatur Rd. Turn right on Crane St.; Butler Tree Farm will be on the left.

John & Dede Howard Recreation Trail

St. Joseph, MI 49085

Bike, walk or drive to Lake Court and enjoy a scenic view of Lake Michigan from the pedestrian bridge. At the bottom of the wooden switchback bridge lies the southern end of the John & Dede Howard Recreation Trail. Whether by day or night you'll find this to be a great stroll or bike ride for the whole family. This end of the trail is well-lit for night strolls and you'll find many benches along the tree-lined path. During our spring visit we encountered bluejays, cardinals, a woodpecker and a little bird enjoying a dust bath. From this location you'll find yourself close enough to Lions Park Beach to take a quick, refreshing dip in the lake before moving on. This beach also offers the nearest restroom until you make it all the way to the north end of Silver Beach.

At Park Street you'll head toward the Lake and stroll along sandy Silver Beach. This section of the trail is quite busy in the summer months and the sidewalk runs alongside busy Lake Street so be certain your group is aware of vehicles. The trail curves east past the Silver Beach Carousel, Whirlpool Fountain and Curious Kids Discovery Museum. If you manage to keep your group from the quality distractions provided, cross the railroad tracks and stay to the left on Vine Street.

Here the trail joins the Margaret S. Upton Arboretum and will likely become a bit less congested. Along this shady stretch you'll enjoy sculptures installed by the Krasl Art Center, plenty of quiet picnic locations (bring a blanket), and great views of the St. Joseph River. Keep your eyes out for the ducks who may be uninvited guests to your picnic. If your timing is right, you may enjoy a train crossing the swing bridge, or a barge docking at Lafarge Corporation on the north bank of the river. Please note restrooms are not available along the Arboretum. You may wish to continue east past State Street as the trail continues until the Bicentennial Bridge at the base of the Berrien County Courthouse.

Parking to access the trail is available on Lake Court, at Lions Park Beach, at Silver Beach and at the base of State Street along the St. Joseph River. If you don't expect your group to make it along the trail and back again, you may wish to park one car at each end. Much of the trail is without shade, so be sure to carry water and wear sun protection.

Kal-Haven Trail

Trailhead locations where passes can be purchased:

Kalamazoo (East)
10th Street Staging Area (North of WH Ave.) - Daily Passes & Annual Passes
10th Street
Kalamazoo, MI 49009

South Haven (West)
South Haven Staging Area (North of Wells Street) - Daily Passes & Annual Passes
Bailey Street
South Haven, MI 49090

Bloomingdale:
Trail staff are stationed by the old depot - Daily Passes & Annual Passes
At the intersection of Kalamazoo Street and Van Buren Street
Bloomingdale, MI 49026

8 am to 10 p.m. daily

A favorite bike ride of ours is the Kal-Haven trail. The trail is built on the abandoned Kalamazoo & South Haven Railroad, which existed from 1870 to 1970. It is 33.5 miles long running from Kalamazoo to South Haven. Since the trail is an old rail line it is fairly flat and fairly straight. The trail is 10 feet wide and the surface is crushed slag and limestone. For the most part it is relatively smooth, making it nice for biking, jogging, hiking, and walking. There is a section between Kibble and Bloomingdale where horseback riding is allowed on an adjacent trial next to main trail. Snowmobiling is also allowed when the snow depth is greater than 4 inches. The trail goes through heavily wooded areas and open farmland, as well as several streams and small bodies of water, all of which allow for opportunities to see various types of birds and other wild life.

Trail passes are required for use of the trail. A day pass is $3 for an individual and $7 for a family; the annual pass is a great deal if you use the trail more more than five times a year. There are three staffed locations on the trail for purchasing tickets. These are at the trailheads in Kalamazoo and South

Kal-Haven Trail (cont.)

Haven, as well as in Bloomingdale at the Bloomingdale Depot Trail Station. There is also a list on the Kal-Haven website of vendors who also sell the trail passes. Parking is available at both trailhead locations, as well at Grand Junction, Bloomingdale and Gobles. Camping is available at various locations along the trail, check Kal-Haven website for details.

Personally we like to start in South Haven and ride to Grand Junction, which is approximately 10 miles. In Grand Junction is the Country Fare Restaurant just off the trail. We like to stop and get a bite to eat and then turn around and ride back to South Haven. It is a nice ride, and makes a nice family outing. We will sometimes go into downtown South Haven afterwards and get an ice cream at Dairy Queen to cap off the day.

Starting in South Haven at the trailhead, water and restrooms are available. Other amenities are as follows:
Mile 4 in Kibbie -- picnic site and restrooms
Mile 7 in Lacota -- picnic site and restrooms
Mile 10 in Grand Junction -- water, picnic site and restrooms
Mile 14 -- picnic site
Mile 16 in Bloomingdale -- water, picnic site and restrooms
Mile 20 in Gobles --water, picnic site and restrooms
Mile 26 -- picnic site and restrooms
Mile 29 in Alamo -- picnic site and restrooms
Mile 33 in Kalamazoo -- water, picnic site and restrooms

Potato Creek Campground

25601 Indiana State Road 4
North Liberty, IN 46554-9011
574-656-8186
866-622-6746
www.in.gov/dnr/parklake/2972.htm

Camping families love to stay at Potato Creek. The campground is located well inside the spacious park, so enjoy the scenic drive. This is a popular campground, so make reservations online at www.camp.in.gov or by phone up to a month in advance. We would not recommend showing up without a reservation in the warmer months. Potato Creek has miles of hiking trails and and paved biking trails of varying difficulties. As you travel the trails, you'll

Potato Creek Campground (cont.)

encounter a nature center, lake, boat rental facility and campground store.

The nature center runs daily presentations, as well as arts and crafts projects that elementary school children particularly enjoy. The center has dioramas and displays of the local flora and fauna that you may find in the park. The lake has a swimming beach with a sandy bottom in the shallows, transitioning to mud further out. At the beach, you will find a volleyball court (bring your own ball, no reservations required) and benches in both sunny and shady spots. The concession stand sells snacks and cold drinks; enjoy them at the nearby picnic tables. There are bathrooms and showering facilities at the beach location.

The boat rental is located on a separate part of the lake, about a mile away, so plan accordingly. You can rent paddle boats, canoes, and flat bottom fishing boats. Bring your driver's license or leave a cash deposit. The lake doesn't permit motorized boats. Life jackets and seat cushions come with the boat rental, and the rates are quite reasonable. The lake is small, so an hour's rental will give you time to make a trip all the way around, looking at the wildlife on the banks.

The store is very well stocked. You can bike to the store and leave your bike in the outdoor rack. The store is where you can rent bicycles to enjoy all the trails, as well as purchase wood for your campfire. The store staff has been very thoughtful in stocking everything a camper might forget - ketchup for your hot dogs, graham crackers for your s'mores, and toothpaste for your toothbrush. You do pay a premium for the convenience, but the store is an excellent amenity in case you have left behind a critical item.

Kids with excess energy after all the boating, biking and walking will be able to burn it off at the play area located centrally within the spread of campsites. There are swings, monkeybars, slides, and tons of room to run around. The campsites are close together and relatively small. Although the park itself is wooded, shade and privacy within the camping area is at a premium. Fortunately, there are so many activities within the park, you won't find yourself spending much of the day at your campsite. Quiet hours are from 11 p.m. to 6 am. Alcohol is not permitted in the park. Pets must be kept on a leash at all times.

Directions: From US-31 take Mayflower Road exit. Turn right on Mayflower Road. The road name changes to Sumption Trail, and then to Oak Road. Turn right onto Osborne Road. Veer left to remain on Osborne. Turn right at Pine Rd.

Warren Dunes State Park

Sawyer, MI 49106
269-426-4613

Open year-round
Per-car charge to enter

Beautiful Warren Dunes State Park offers three miles of shoreline, six miles of hiking trails and a dune formation that rises 260 feet above the lake, offering spectacular views of the lake and park. The park also includes a fabulous campground.

To camp at Warren Dunes, either reserve a spot in advance online or by phone, or just show up and take your chances. Campsites are small to medium-sized, equipped with fire rings. RV hookups are available on some sites. The bathrooms are nice and include showering facilities. Near the bathrooms is a play area, including monkey bars, slides and a sandbox. Bring a flying disc or football as there is a lot of room to throw and catch. You park your car in front of your campground. There are also rustic campsites (no bathroom or electric hookups, but pump water). Highway noises from nearby I-94 can be very noticeable, especially at night.

Walking trails start near the campsites, including a 2 1/2 mile trail that takes you to a beach. There are no lifeguards at Warren Dunes, and there is frequently a strong undertow. There have been a number of drownings, so please use caution. In the winter Warren Dunes' hiking trails are transformed into miles of cross-country skiing trails.

Hiking up the dunes is terrific fun. This is physically demanding, and in the summer sun it can be a hot and taxing trip. Avoid flip-flops or sandals, which can be hard to drag through the sand. At the top of the dune is a small grove of trees. Bring a strong and sturdy rope and hang a rope swing for the kids (and adults) to swing from and jump off onto the sandy hillside. If you don't have a rope, rolling down the dunes is always a popular alternative with the younger set. Be prepared to brush off lots of sand before you get back in your car!

Directions: From I-94, take exit 16 toward Bridgman. Turn right on Red Arow Highway, then make a sharp right on Hildebrandt Rd.

INTRODUCTION

Montessori education extends beyond the classroom from a young age. Primary students at Brookview go on nature walks and participate in the feeding of our two sheep, Snowy and Midnight. Elementary students identify community resources that can help them further explore their own interests. They then plan the excursion, taking responsibility for their own learning. The varied events in this chapter take place outside of Berrien County, but we think they're well worth the extra travel time. We encourage you to involve your kids in planning the outings. Next time they ask "Are we there yet?" hand them the map and have them figure it out for themselves!

Hesston Steam Train Museum

1201 E 1000 N, La Porte IN
219-872-5055
www.hesston.org

Open weekends
Memorial Day - Labor Day 11:30am - 5pm CENTRAL TIME

Special holiday trains run weekends in October and December; check website for details.

Kids young and old love to ride the trains at the Hesston Steam Train Museum. There are trains in both 1/4 scale and the very small 1/8 scale. Located just over the Indiana state line, the trains run a 2 1/2 mile track through woods and fields. Trains run weekends and holidays throughout the summer and fall. Purchase tickets at the station for each member of your party; children under three ride free. The tickets are printed on handsome cardstock and make neat souvenirs. Rides last about ten minutes, and there is a conductor on board who can answer questions about the trains. There are also a few specialty trains. The Haunted Train ride at the end of October is mildly scary; sensitive under-fours may find a few things startling. The Candy Cane express in December runs in an enclosed coach, which helps keep faces and fingers unfrozen. Santa is there to greet the travellers.

The grounds around the museum have lots of machinery for train lovers to explore. There is a working steam-driven sawmill (which runs only on special occasions) and you can walk through an original caboose from the

Hesston Steam Train Museum (cont.)

South Shore Line, which used to take vacationers from Chicago to Southwestern Michigan. There are also other antique engines in various states of repair. There is no enclosed museum building, but the gift shop has a small display of photographs and other train artifacts. They also carry Thomas toys, DVDs of trains and other machinery, and train dress-up items. There is a big selection of enameled lapel pins with historical train logos.

There are often several snack and lunch options. Picnic tables are scattered around, many shaded, and picnickers are welcome. The Snack Shack offers the usual hot dogs and nachos, but also a few more interesting dishes such as homemade tamales and aloe tea. Esther's Kitchen is open sporadically and offers authentic pierogies, Polish sausage and soft pretzels. The real draw in the fall is the freshly pressed cider, which you can buy by the gallon or by the heated cupful. The cider is unpasteurized, so decide in advance if it's something you want to offer the younger children in your party.

Bathrooms are cinderblock and a short walk from the main station building. There is ample parking. The museum is on Central Time, so make sure to adjust your plans accordingly.

Directions: Take I-94 to exit 1, MI-239, heading south. Turn left onto W 1000 Rd North. The turn to the museum is on your left and is well-marked with a large billboard.

Kalamazoo Air Zoo

6151 Portage Road
Portage, MI 49002
269-382-6555
www.airzoo.org

Monday - Saturday 9 am - 5 pm (East campus opens at 11 am)
Sunday noon - 5 pm
Closed Thanksgiving, Christmas eve, and Christmas Day

If the roads are clear, but the weather is gloomy, there are always blue skies up I-94 at the Kalamazoo Air Zoo. Kids and adults alike who are interested in flight will have a great time exploring the two huge hangars that hold the museum's impressive collection. Head first to the Main Campus building. Make sure to look up as you enter the lobby - there are a number of small aircraft on display up above. The lobby also houses the large museum gift shop,

Kalamazoo Air Zoo (cont.)

specializing in cool science toys and models, as well as T-shirts and bomber jackets. Take advantage of the coat check - you won't want to deal with bulky jackets on all the rides. If you have a toddler, keep your stroller - the Air Zoo requires a lot of walking, and little legs get tired. The entrance into the main display space is a twisting tunnel painted with very realistic sky and clouds.

The display area is enormous. It is very cool to see an F-14 Tomcat and a Blackbird spy plane up close. Many museum guides are retired military who flew these planes in action; they are happy to share their extensive knowledge, and their love for the planes is obvious. Once you enter, to your left is a side space with toys and rides for toddlers. Follow the yellow path around the hangar to make sure you don't miss anything. The planes are laid out in roughly chronological order - fragile little biplanes to the left, WWI and WWII planes in the center, and modern jets on the right. The walls are decorated with the world's largest indoor mural, commemorating milestones in flight. Don't neglect the room holding relics and documents on the Battle of Guadalcanal. There's an open cockpit to keep little kids busy while you read over the fascinating story of this important battle.

Where the Air Zoo really shines is in the rides. These require a separate ticket; if you're planning to spend more than a few hours, an unlimited ride pass is a good deal. Otherwise, rides are a few dollars each. Like the rest of the museum, the rides cover the historical span of manned flight. You can start with the carnival-like rides in a hot air balloon or a biplane that moves up and down as it flies in a circle. These rides are appropriate for smaller children, and they're thoughtfully placed near the Kid's Korner play space. Older children will have a great time on the flight simulators, and they're almost as fun to watch in action as they are to ride. Each is a closed box, and once the ride is activated, the box lifts, leans, and spins around on powerful hydraulic arms. Whole families can enter the Space Shuttle ride.

Once you've explored the Main Campus, grab some lunch at the Kitty Hawk cafe on the second floor. They sell burgers, sandwiches, pizza and hot dogs. Then make sure not to miss the East Campus, which is just as large. Here, the focus is on space exploration. Kids can get strapped into an elastic harness, like a huge jumperoo, to try out their "space legs" in a simulated low-gravity environment. Check out a real astronaut's spacesuit, a mockup of the shuttle kitchen, and look at a genuine Moon rock. The East campus also holds the museum collection of WWII naval planes. Finally, if you need a break

Kalamazoo Air Zoo (cont.)

(it's a lot of walking in these huge buildings!) there's an Observation Lounge with a great view of real planes taking off and landing at Kalamazoo/ Battle Creek International Airport.

Directions: Drive on I-94 east towards Detroit. Take exit 78, Portage Rd, and turn right to travel south. After you cross E. Milham Ave, make a left onto the Air Zoo campus. The parking lot will be to the left of the building.

Kalamazoo Valley Museum

230 N. Rose Street
Kalamazoo, MI 49003
269-373-7990
www.kalamazoomuseum.org

Monday - Thursday 9 am - 5 pm
Friday 9 am - 10 pm
Saturday 9 am - 5 pm
Sunday and holidays 1 pm - 5 pm
Closed Easter, Thanksgiving, Christmas Eve and Christmas

The Kalamazoo Valley Museum is well worth a day trip to Kalamazoo for kids of all ages. This is a terrific museum packed with attractions to keep everyone busy. The focus is on hands-on learning about history, science, and technology. The exhibits are well thought-out, engaging, and kept in good order. Best of all, admission to the Museum is free! Consider combining a trip here with the Kalamazoo Air Zoo if you have older kids; younger ones will be tired out with just one of these attractions.

When you enter, make sure to get a map of exhibits at the visitor's desk. The center of the museum is a three-story escalator that allows you to see the towering display of objects from Kalamazoo's history. Stop at each landing to read the descriptions of this interesting potpourri of objects, and play "I Spy." The first floor has an unsecured cloakroom, and small lockers for valuables require a quarter to activate. Towards the back is the Plantetarium, and some wonderul hands-on weather exhibits. Spin a giant water-filled cylinder to create a tornado, or play with sand as it is jostled into dunes. The Planetarium requires a $3 ticket; while the schedule varies daily, there is usually a show at 3 pm.

The second floor of the museum has an excellent space devoted to simple mechanics. One of the most popular exhibits for older kids (and parents) is the

Kalamazoo Valley Museum (cont.)

chance to build your own race car, then guide it around the electrified track. The museum staff do a wonderful job keeping the exhibits working and they have some very creative displays. The back of the second floor has a dedicated play space for kids five and under. Here you'll find special activites geared towards the younger set, a nice library with cozy reading nooks, and some buildings for imaginary play. This section of the museum is walled off so it's easy to let your toddlers roam without worry of losing them. The remainder of the second floor will be undergoing renovations throughout 2010; the updated display on local history is eagerly anticipated.

The third floor holds rotating special exhibits. On a recent visit, the subject was robotics. Our kids loved challenging a robot arm to a game of Tangrams, programming virtual creatures, and the pictorial display of both imaginary and real robots throughout the years. The special exhibits are well thought-out and very high quality. While you're on the third floor, make sure not to miss the Egyptian room, where kids are always fascinated by the two real mummies (one a queen, one a cat) on display. A series of models illustrates how the queen may have appeared when alive. The third floor also has the Stryker Theater, the site of movies, lectures, and live performances most days of the week. Check the website for theater details before you go; the information can be a little hard to find in the museum itself. Some of the events require tickets.

Directions: Take I-94E to exit 76B, Westnedge Ave, heading north. After about 2.3 miles, veer right onto S Park St. Turn right on W Michigan Ave, then take the second left onto N Rose St. The Kalamazoo Valley Museum will be on your right. There is a public parking garage on the next block.

Kee-Boon-Mein-Kaa Pow Wow

58620 Sink Rd
Dowagiac MI 49047
www.pokagonpowwow.com

Labor Day Weekend

The Pokagon band hosts an annual pow wow on their tribal lands every Labor Day. Kee-Boon-Mein-Kaa refers to the end of the huckleberry harvest. Today, this celebration includes ceremonial dancers, singers, drum circles, food and craft vendors and more. One of the highlights of the pow wow is the dance competition. Women and men compete separately in several different

Kee-Boon-Mein-Kaa Pow Wow (cont.)

categories. The male traditional dancers tell stories through their movements, recounting hunts and battles of old. The women's traditional dance is also rich in symbolic meaning, and their regalia is quite intricate and beautiful. It is worth spending a little time researching online or in the library before you go, so you can better appreciate what you're seeing. Men and women also compete in their respective fancy dance categories, marked by high jumps from the men and twirling shawls from the women. The Grand Entries occur several times throughout the weekend and mark the formal start of the dancing; these are highlights of the pow wow and you should be sure to attend at least one. You can watch the dancers from the grandstands, which are sheltered from the sun. The benches are backless, but you can bring cushions. Some people set up lawn chairs in a small grassy area, but this fills up quickly.

Since the dancing usually starts after lunch, plan to spend the morning looking at some of the wonderful crafts at the vendor booths. Many serious artisans come to display their work, all of them producing Native-made crafts. You can purchase black ash baskets, beadwork, and leather items such as bags or barrettes. There are also pieces of regalia for the dancers and drum makers for musicians. Members of tribes across North America attend, so there are usually some southwestern crafts such as silver and turquoise jewelry and woven blankets. Many of the vendors accept credit cards. Some artisans will present morning workshops. Sign up early for the chance to try your hand at basket making; if you don't get to participate, you're still welcome to watch.

The pow wow is also a chance to sample traditional foods. Fry bread comes in a number of styles, including sweetened with honey and cinnamon, as well as served as an "Indian taco" with cheese and meat toppings. You'll find dishes made with buffalo and venison, as well as corn soup. Make sure to sample the fresh squeezed lemonade that many food vendors serve, or try some traditional root and herb teas such as sassafras. No alcohol is permitted at the pow wow. Meals are eaten in a large tent with plenty of seating.

Everyone is invited to attend Kee-Boon-Mein-Kaa Pow Wow and there is no admission or parking charge. Please take the time to visit the website and learn about the proper etiquette for this ceremonial event. The competitors are not performers; they are dancers and are referred to as such. Similarly, they wear regalia, not costumes. Make sure to ask permission before taking photographs of the dancers or singers. During certain points in the ceremony, everyone stands quietly and removes their hat. Listen for the PA announcements or pay

Kee-Boon-Mein-Kaa Pow Wow (cont.)

attention to the way the elders behave. If you come with a respectful manner, you will be very welcome.

The parking area is about a half mile walk to the dance arena, but there are golf carts and people movers, towed by tractors, if you need a ride. Porta Potties and several bathhouses are available.

Directions: From I-94, take exit 27, Pipestone Rd, heading east and quickly merge onto Meadowbrook Rd. Travel 8 miles, then make a right onto MI-140 S. Drive 6.5 miles, then turn left at MI-62 E. After 3.7 miles, make a right on Sink Rd. The entrance to tribal lands will be 2.7 miles down, on your right.

Old Fashioned Christmas Celebration

Downtown Dowagiac
www.dowagiacchamber.com

Christmas Open House:
Weekend before Thanksgiving

Candlelight Christmas Parade:
First Friday in December at 7 pm

Dowagiac pulls out all the stops to celebrate Christmas in the downtown business district. Things kick off with the Christmas Open House, held the weekend prior to Thanksgiving. Retailers hold an open house beginning on Friday, but the real family fun starts Saturday at 10 am. Kids can visit with an Old World Santa, who held court indoors at a local restaurant in 2009. For a nominal fee, take a horse-drawn carriage ride through downtown, and pet Santa's live reindeer. Beckwith Park holds music and dance performances, while the Theta Mu sorority runs a craft show of about forty vendors in the high school from 9 am to 2 pm. Parking is available in several city lots or on the streets in the business district. Area merchants stay open and many offer snacks, and the local restaurants do a brisk business for lunch and dinner. Public bathrooms can be found at the Historic Train Depot, on Depot Drive between Park and Commerical Streets.

Return to Dowagiac several weeks later for the Annual Candlelight Christmas parade. This is a large parade with over 100 entries, including floats, marching bands, and community groups. All entrants are encouraged to use light decorations, including garlands of Christmas lights and hand-carried candles.

Old Fashioned Christmas Celebration (cont.)

The parade starts at the corner of Front and Main, and makes a loop through downtown Dowagiac. After travelling up Front Street, the route turns on to Division Drive, and then up to Depot Drive. Street vendors sell cocoa and spiced cider, while the floats often feature a candy cane toss as they travel the route. The Grandstand for dignitaries and parade judges is in front of Beckwith park at Front and Beeson Streets; this is a particularly good place to see the bands perform their best pieces. The parade moves quickly because it can be quite cold; expect it to last about 25 minutes. People start parking as early as 2 pm - the lots on Depot Drive are popular, and it's common to park your car so you can sit on the back for a good view. Otherwise, people stand on the sidewalks or between the parked cars; no bleachers are provided.

Directions: From US-31, take exit 18, Tabor Road, headed east. Tabor Road will dead-end into Pipestone Road; make a right. Pipestone Road becomes W Main Street as you travel through Eau Claire, then becomes M-62. As you enter Dowagiac, M-62 merges with M-51 and is again called Main Street. Make a left at the merge and you will travel into downtown Dowagiac.

Potawatomi Park Zoo

500 S. Greenlawn Avenue
South Bend, IN 46615
574-235-9080
www.potawatomizoo.org

Open April - November daily 10 am - 5 pm CENTRAL TIME
Closed December - March

Indiana's oldest zoo is home to more than 400 animals. Popular attractions include the Australian walkabout, which has kangaroos and wallabies, and the red panda exhibit. The Zoo Farm is a nice twist on the usual farm animals - this one displays farm animals from different continents. Instead of cows and sheep, you may find alpacas or Nubian goats. The zoo expanded their lion habitat in recent years, and also boasts two different rare leopard species. Last year, the zoo debuted a living Butterfly collection, which will return for 2010.

One highlight of a trip to the Potawatomi Zoo is the train ride. An old-fashioned engineer makes the ride a fun-filled learning experience for young and old. You can purchase tickets at the front office, or pay cash at the start of the ride. Also, make sure to bring some coins to get a handful of fish food. The fish are

Potawatomi Park Zoo (cont.)

extremely enthusiastic to get the little pellets and will make quite a splash as they jostle each other about! The zoo is one part of Potawatomi Park, which includes a softball diamond, tennis courts, a swimming pool, picnic area, band shell, and Kid's Kingdom Playground. The playground is huge, with lots of climbing, and a soft rubberized surface. Be careful, as it can be easy to lose track of your kids to the surrounding fields.

Don't forget to stop by the Learning Center, where you can see smaller animals in terrariums. Your kids might have a close encounter with a chinchilla or a blue-tongued skink. The Learning Center also hosts birthday parties and various day classes and camps. Visit their website for details and live feeds from the zoo cams. Admission to the zoo is $7.50 for adults and $5.50 for children 2 - 14. There are additional charges for train rides, pony rides, and visits to the butterfly exhibit.

The Potawatomi Zoo's Congo Cafe serves panini sandwiches and grilled items. We appreciate the recent addition of milk and juice to the menu. Browse the Jungle Gift Shop for animal-themed toys. There's an ATM in case you run out of cash. Alternatively, the park across the street has some picnic tables, so you could pack your own meal to enjoy after walking through the zoo.

Directions: From US-31, continue on US-20. Take the South Bend/North Liberty exit. Turn left on IN-23 North. Turn right on W. Samples Street. Continue to follow IN-23. Bear left on IN-23 North. Turn right on Sunnymeade Avenue. Turn right on S. Greenlaw Avenue. Arrive at the Potawatomi Zoo on the left.

Turkeyville USA

18935 15-1/2 Mile Road
Marshall, MI 49068
269-781-4293
www.turkeyville.com

Open 11 am - 8 pm daily
Check website for date and times of special events

Turkeyville makes a great day trip. It's a little hard to categorize this attraction, which is located just off I-69, between Kalamazoo and Ann Arbor. It is a working farm and raises turkeys. They have a large dining hall where you can get a wide range of turkey dishes, like their incredible turkey sandwiches, turkey soup, and slices of smoked turkey. Each week before Thanksgiving they sell

Turkeyville USA (cont.)

fresh turkeys ranging from 12 to 35 pounds. There's also an ice cream parlor and a sweet shop selling homemade fudge and old-fashioned hard candy. But Turkeyville has a lot more than just great food, which is what makes it an attractive trip for families with younger kids.

Check out the website or call ahead to find out what days the trains are running. The Mid-Michigan Railroad Club meets at Turkeyville several times during the year and runs their trains on the 1/8 scale track. The trains are a hobby for these families and are powered by coal, kerosene, or wood. 1/8 scale trains are quite small - think engines no more than three feet high - and you often perch on top of a boxcar as you ride around the track. Trains cross over a trestle, go through a tunnel, and pass the roundhouse where the hobbyists work. Rides leave frequently, so even when there is a line, it moves pretty fast. The club requests a nominal donation for each ride.

Turkeyville also hosts some wonderful craft fairs, drawing vendors from around the state. Emphasis is on handmade items such as children's clothing, room decor and jewelry as well as some unique handcrafted items. Nothing is very expensive and it's fun to browse the booths. Again, check the website or call ahead for dates for the fairs.

The dining hall gets very crowded - buses arrive at Turkeyville pretty frequently. It's a smart idea to have one adult wait in line while another watches the kids and finds a picnic space. Tables are at a premium, but if you bring a picnic blanket you'll have lots of green space to choose from. Try the field that leads down to the trains and watch them pass by as you eat. After lunch, burn off some energy on the small climbing structures and swings. There are also some farm animals to see, including turkeys, chickens and assorted small livestock.

If you're lucky, Turkeyville sometimes hosts ultra-light plane enthusiasts, who land in a field beyond the big parking area. They can get hidden behind a hill, but if you happen to see any, it's worth your while to walk over and take a look. Most of them are gracious to kids and will explain a little about their machines. It's amazing to see how small and delicate the planes are up close.

Campers enjoy Turkeyville and there is space set aside for them. There's a dinner theater too. Tickets for dinner and a show are $38.50, with no children's tickets available. Still, older children that can eat quietly and enjoy the show should find it fun.

Directions: Take I-94E, towards Detroit, to exit 108 onto I-69N. Travel four miles, then take exit 42, N Drive N, and make a left. Turkeyville will be on your left; make a left onto 15 1/2 Mile Dr. There are large signs to show you where to park.

INTRODUCTION

This chapter covers attractions that we just couldn't shoehorn into other categories, but were too cool to leave out. Give them a try - we think you'll agree, they deserved their own chapter.

Bridge to China Language School

Saint Joseph High School
2521 Stadium Drive
St. Joseph, MI 49085
www.bridgetochina.org

Fall semester: September - December
Winter/Spring semester: January - May

Berrien County families have a chance to learn both Mandarin Chinese and written Chinese at the non-profit Bridge to China program. Bridge to China holds classes at the Saint Joseph high school. Their curriculum starts with a preschool level class for 2-3 year olds and their parents, where toddlers get exposure to Chinese through songs, rhymes, and other fun circle-time activities. There are two levels of the Chinese as a Second Language classes for older kids; more experienced children then move on to the Mandarin Chinese classes, which are immersion classes. Adults have a chance to participate in conversation classes, or to learn about business-specific cultural concerns in evening classes. Bridge to China sometimes offers events for the community, such as a Chinese New Year celebration or a trip to Chinatown. Check their website for more details.

Directions: From I-94, take exit 27, Niles Rd, towards St. Joseph. Take a left on Hilltop Ave, then a right on Cleveland Ave, which will merge with Lakeshore Dr. You'll pass the football stadium; make a right on Wallace Ave and an immediate right on Stadium Dr to reach the high school.

Whirlpool Compass Fountain

Silver Beach
St. Joseph, MI 49085
www.sjtoday.org

Runs daily from May - mid-October
noon - 2 pm and 5 pm - 10 pm

The Whirlpool Compass Fountain debuted in September 2009, just behind Silver Beach. More than a decoration, the fountain basin is barrier free, inviting kids and adults alike to walk on in and get wet. Water shoots up from the ground in 28 different jets. Little kids who step on a jet and look down are apt to get a faceful of water if their foot moves. Eight spheres on wrought iron posts circle the 150ft diameter fountain. Every fifteen minutes, the water cannons hidden inside these spheres shoot water 35 feet up in the air. At night, the fountain is lit up with various lighting programs. It's a beautiful addition to the attractions below the Bluff. If the lake water is too cold to enjoy, hike over to the Compass Fountain for some outdoors water play.

Michiana Rocketry

Three Oaks, MI 49128
www.michianarocketry.org

Attending a model rocket launch event is a perfect activity on a sunny winter weekend. It is fun for kids and parents alike. Michiana Rocketry is a local club devoted to flying model rockets. The club is connected to the little Red Arrow Hobby Shop situated near the 5 O'clock Sports Bar at I-94's exit 23. The launch field itself is east of Three Oaks, Michgan in several square miles of corn fields. For this reason, the monthly launches are fall through spring when the crops fields are empty.

Launch pads are installed at different levels of distance so you can fly your own $20 starter-kit rocket, but they also fly serious toys like ten-feet-tall power rockets with multi-stage propulsion engines that will propel them up to 16,000 feet (field is covered by special FAA clearance on those days) before they gently parachute down to the ground. For most, the fun is in the watching. No entrance fee required. Sounds and smoke are guaranteed. It may scare a baby for a few seconds, but not enough to make you reconsider a visit.

Michiana Rocketry (cont.)

Launches are continuous through the day with some unpredictable periods of inactivity. You can of course bring a chair and watch all day, but the occasional curious visitor should plan to stay around for two hours to walk around, watch launches of different power and talk to owners of the large rockets who proudly display them in their custom-fitted vans and trucks, and are always ready for a friendly chat.

It can get really cold on those winter days with the breeze in the open fields. Make sure you come sufficiently dressed. While Michiana Rocketry is really friendly to all visitors, it is also not very busy and not very commercial. Some folks will sell rocket starter-kits and spare parts from the back of their truck but do not expect any souvenirs, food stands or picnic tables. There are also no bathrooms. The launch field is at the end of a dirt road and you can park on the side of the road along the launch field. There is a yearly calendar but dates can change up to a few days in advance if weather conditions are bad. Check the website for updated launch dates.

Directions: From I-94, take exit 4 east towards Three Oaks/Niles. Continue east past Three Oaks two miles, turn south on Avery Road. After about 1.5 miles, watch on your right for vehicles out in the corn fields. Turn right on the farm road just before the drainage ditch. If you are driving west on US 12, Avery Road is about 4 miles west of Galien.

St. Joseph Fire Station

923 South Broad St.
St. Joseph, MI 49085
269-983-1442

Open year-round

The firefighters on duty at the station in downtown Saint Joseph are proud of their department's long history, and of their ongoing service to our community. Both of these are on display at the fire station. Little kids will be thrilled to have a tour. The firefighters are terrific as they show off their shiny trucks (washed daily) and let the kids sit in the driver's seat, watch the lights flash, and check out all the gear. Many kids are tongue-tied to meet these genuine heroes, but any questions they have will be answered enthusiastically. There's no need to call ahead or make an appointment - just drop by and ask if it's

St. Joseph Fire Station (cont.)

it's a good time for a tour. In addition to the trucks, our kids have enjoyed seeing the dormitories where the firefighters sleep, and the dummy they use while practicing rescues.

The halls of the fire station display the unit's history. Photographs dating back to 1900 show the old fire station, now home to the Broad Street Cafe. You can see the old-fashioned uniforms and the horse-drawn fire wagons. Prized artifacts, such as a bell from a 1920's truck, an 1870 hay hoist used to feed the station's horses, and one of the original brass poles, are some of the collection's highlights. There are also documents from one of the great tragedies in the Twin Cities' history, the Opera House fire in Benton Harbor. Eleven firemen died battling the blaze in 1896, and their names are still carefully preserved on a shard of glass from the Opera House. It is here that you can learn more about the monument to the fallen firemen, which still stands in Lake Bluff Park, just north of the Maids of the Mist fountain. The Opera House tragedy was nationwide news, and donations from all over the country built the monument. It is believed to be the first or second monument in America to feature electric lights, which cost $2,000 in 1898 - a substantial sum. Read the framed newspapers collected at the fire station, then take a short drive across Main Street to Lake Bluff Park to see the monument, and remember those that continue to risk their lives for us all.

Directions: From Main St in St. Joseph, turn onto Broad St travelling away from Lake Michigan. The fire station will be three blocks down, on your right. You can park in the small lot in front of the station. Don't block the trucks.

Santa's House

Corner of State St. and Pleasant St.
Downtown St. Joseph

December:
Thursday 4 pm - 7 pm, Friday 4 pm - 6 pm
Saturday noon - 5 pm, Sunday 1 pm - 4 pm

Santa arrives in Saint Joseph during the annual Reindog Parade, held in the beginning of December. Kids can come and recite their Christmas lists in his little red and green house, which sits at the corner of State Street and Pleasant Street in downtown St. Joseph. If Santa's not available, there's a mail slot where kids can drop off their letters.

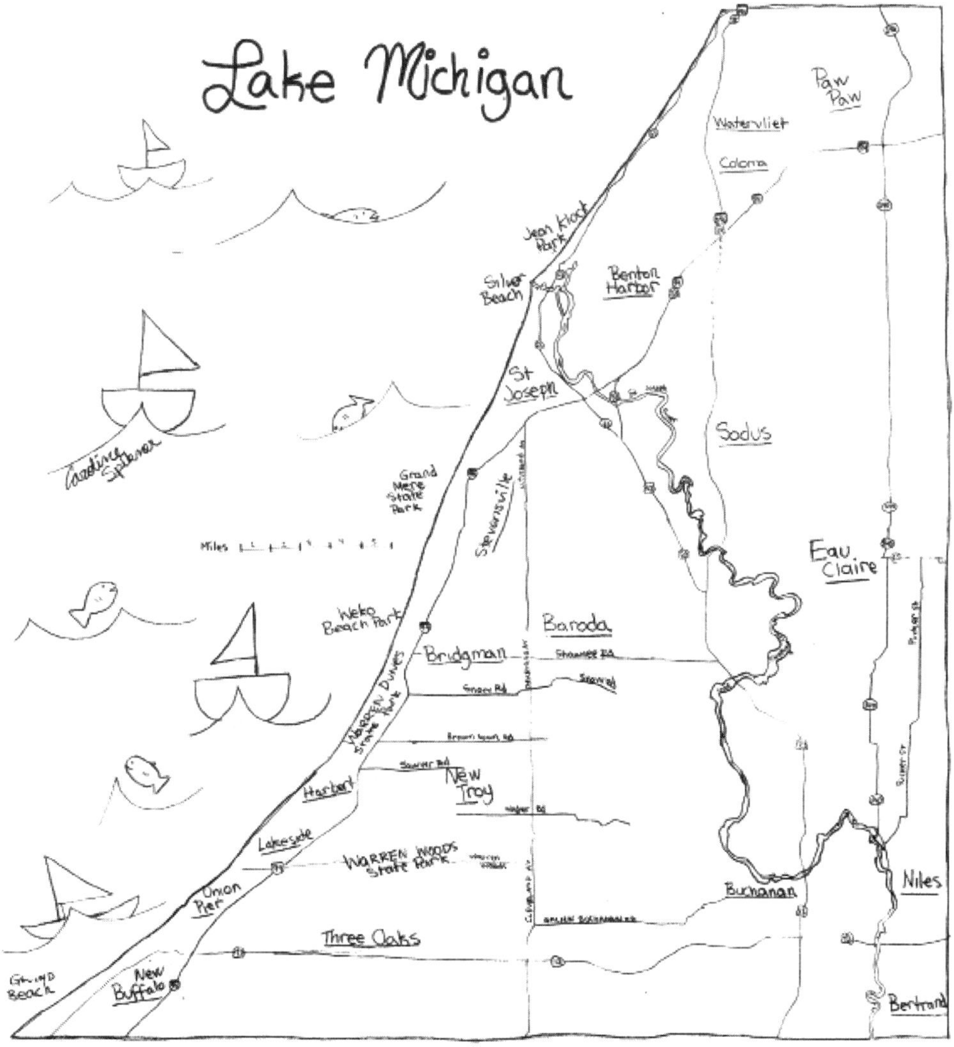

Map by Caroline Spikner
Brookview student

NOTES:

Index

Index by Location

NOTES: